THE
BLUE STAR PORTAL
OF TRANSFORMATION

A Journey of Celph Discovery

Rev. Charla J. Hermann
Grandmother Blue Otter

AuthorHouse™
1663 Liberty Drive, Suite 200
Bloomington, IN 47403
www.authorhouse.com
Phone: 1-800-839-8640

©2009 Rev. Charla J. Hermann. All rights reserved.

No part of this book may be reproduced, stored in a retrieval system, or transmitted by any means without the written permission of the author.

First published by AuthorHouse 4/14/2009

ISBN: 978-1-4389-5478-3 (sc)

Library of Congress Control Number: 2009902263

Printed in the United States of America
Bloomington, Indiana

This book is printed on acid-free paper.

Knew Vision Productions
P.O. Box 70
Valley Head, Al. 35989

www.hawkwindrenews.com

Hawkwind@bellsouth.net
bluestartimes@me.com
http://web.me.com/Bluestartimes

CONTENTS

JOURNEY ONE	*Igniting the Blue Star Spirit*	*1*
JOUNREY TWO	*The Wake up call*	*21*
JOURNEY THREE	*Compassion in the Air*	*27*
JOURNEY FOUR	*Courage of the Heart*	*51*
JOURNEY FIVE	*Creating a safe container for TRUTH beyond FEAR*	*62*
JOURNEY SIX	*Strength comes from Commitment*	*73*
JOURNEY SEVEN	*Endurance of the Magical Journey*	*88*
JOURNEY EIGHT	*Wisdom of knowing Self/Celph*	*96*
JOURNEY NINE	*Healing into Wholeness*	*115*
JOURNEY TEN	*Patience creates Big Medicine*	*134*
JOURNEY ELEVEN	*Tools of Transformation*	*154*
JOURNEY TWELVE	*It's all about FORGIVENESS and GRATITUDE*	*172*

INTRODUCTION

THE BLUE STAR PORTAL OF TRANSFORMATION

As this information makes itself available to our species, it comes to life in the hearts, minds, and souls of each who has aligned with this sacred frequency. Most seekers have, at first, felt to be going through some form of emotional dis-ease, as this information shakes and quakes through the cellular system of all life on this planet. It is a time of extremes and evolution is happening right before our eyes. Light keepers and Medicine practitioners worldwide report the same emotions, dreams, visuals, and inner knowing. Transformation has increased its rate to something akin to warp speed. We are shaking up the Universe to gather the seeds of light and harvest the abundance of information that has been made available to us to access through a series of dedicated frequencies of some COSMIC NEWS NETWORK.

As for getting to know who I am or how I have come to share this with you; it is my honor to have spent over forty years as a reporter and documentarian researching ancient archives of indigenous peoples. I earned that right while serving at the sides of Medicine Elders in ritual and ceremony. I was allowed to access the insights that have been passed on from generation to generation since the early 1700's. Then I was allowed to experience the actual process in order that it might continue to live in my cells of knowing. The process that I went through to access this transformational tool came after Sun Dancing, Ghost Dancing, Questing and participating in hundred and hundreds of sacred rituals, Stone People's lodges and much more. . It came from coming to know the importance of the Spiritual languages and Sacred codes. It was after years of service to the process of transformation that I received it in my own challenged cells. I was asking Spirit for the right to become an active part of the Golden Age, and one day I found myself leading a ceremony for those same Elders who were now passing on the tidbits of life they deemed most important in their own sacred journey. In my heart it is my knowing that *WE ARE THOSE ANICIENT ONES, RETURNED TO COMPLETE A CONTRACT TO SUPPORT THE TRANSFORMATION OF MOTHER EARTH, AND ALL OUR REALTIONS.*

Using a combination of skills that were equally chiseled in the boardrooms of CNN, ABC, and CBS I found my real passion as a Sacred Storyteller. Raised in the spiritual arms of the Wind River Reservation of Wyoming, I was blessed with a unique perspective that honors ancient traditions as well as modern day expression of Shamanism. It is a thrill to assist the old ones in providing their wisdom teachings to thousands as they chose to help us through these tumultuous times. Carrying forward their message has evolved from workshops, newsletters, publications, books, along with the acclaimed documentary series, Quest of the Earth Keepers. Together we weave healing stories with prophecies of our native ancestors.

Born Charla Jo Hermann I have been known by many names and nations. Currently, I have claimed the connection to my own family lineage carried to the United States from Ireland, where I came to know my own Grandmother Blue Otter. I honor that energy as a keeper of Medicine, legend and Sacred Lore. This has manifested as a Ceremonialist for the Clan of the Blue Star Grandmothers, an Alchemical Healing teacher, Spirit Dance intercessor, Lodge leader, Sun Dancer, and keeper of ancient altars of personal and planetary transformation. . This has allowed me through many a gateway to experience the shifts offered to this time of great transition into a New-Clear energy age of wholeness.

Home base is Alabama where Tarwater and I built Hawkwind Earth Renewal Cooperative in 1987. Our spiritual healing and transformative programs are held year round. From that base, this work has now found its way into healing circles all over the world. We share this message of rebirth, renewal and hope as we enter a new paradigm of harmony and cooperation.

The time to shed all that no longer serves us is now. The time to remember our soul's contract of service is NOW. We must come to know ourselves as able to perceive the new frequency of joy that transforms the human spirit.

It is very important that you know that even though my original instructions came from Traditional Native American Grandmothers, the actual completion of the rituals was done with Grandmothers of all nations. The original instruction was to integrate into one heart, one mind of all nations. So while I did some of the initiations of Fire in the reservation way, I also participated in Fire Walks with Edwene Gaines, I did Fire Dance with Jeff and Abby McBride, I did Soul Fire with my Sis-star Mz. Imani. I found my relationship with each element in many ways. With Earth there was the Stone People's lodge, Cannunpa and Medicine Wheel work. There was also work in the pyramids and working with plants around the world. With the water rites I could be found in many forms of purifications. Not all of them were at the waters edges, but involved de-toxing my body and cleaning my blood while working on a series of internal questions that were driving the bus of disease. While working on air, I learned lots of songs and danced in lots of circles, but the air that I came to know as mine and finding a new voice was ever bit as important as the process I went through to make a rattle or dance for days and nights on end in prayer.

How you take this information and integrate it into your world is about you and where you came from. You don't have to do it the way I did. This is a story and a series of process that do not have to follow a special order in doing the rituals for your self. If you don't do it my way, you won't turn into a frog! This series assumes WE are all frogs at some level and we can swim our way to shore with a multitude of instructions. Some don't need all of this to kick them into a new reality. I did, and many of my students have. What I offer here is the culmination of over forty years of training to find the heart and soul of me, and how I got tricked to get here.

This story took me from a life threatening disease, to the day that I stood inside the Great Pyramid in Egypt, celebrating my new life and rebirth into wholeness. I share with you the means that allowed me to rewrite the story within my own cells.

If nothing else, it makes for some smiles and entertainment that it took so much struggle and mystery to get to the place of epiphany of what had always been just a breath of knowing away,

☪

I am Charla Jo Pumpkin, found under an alien rock revived from the ethers, inspired by the ancients, motivated by the suffering children, kite string to the Universe, Shaman from the Stars, to the Stars, Spinner of new life in the primordial waters of creation. I am daughter of space and time. I am Mother of Hope and Keeper of Prophecy. I am Grandmother to the Clan and lover of life. I can see the source of who I am. I am fully present in the act of living!!

☪

DEDICATION

We give this book back to the Star Nation Grandmothers of ancient circles of transformation that held the codes of the Sacred Trust throughout time. Once again, they waited for seven generations to bring this information forward. Now is the time to regenerate our planet and open the gateways to the Golden Age. The help we have requested has arrived. Many of us kept waiting for an old one to knock on the door and tell us that it was time for this change. We haven't been sure what all it meant; this changing of time. We have been trained for it in a thousand ways, yet none of us can guarantee the total effect of the process. We wanted a sign that said NOW.

For us, when it actually happened, we were stunned ,amazed, and quite overwhelmed. One night we received a surprise visit from an old Ute Gram from Colorado. She pulled up after almost three days with her driver. She changed clothes and crawled into the lodge. We were frightened to ask what would make her leave her family and drive straight to us. The voice of this tiny eighty-five year old woman was booming;

"Them Spirits got your resume. You got the job! Now get busy."

For myself, I sat in the darkness pinching myself and wondering if I would remember the job description of what I had applied for in a past life. The fact that I had actually lived long enough to see this time of New-Clear energy to come into our lives was somewhat alarming to my sense of self. In the moment when I most wanted to access every form of magical power that I was sure I had earned; in that moment I felt lame and useless. I could watch the news, read the latest alarming e-mail or simply answer the crisis line at our center. The shifts on the planet were happening way faster than any other time in my life. I felt like a kid who had been sent to my bedroom to clean for the first time. It was such a mess; I had no idea where to start. So, like every good kid, I sat down in the middle of the room and began to focus on the overwhelming part of it all, not the ability to pick up one toy at a time to see the floor again. For me it was not a bedroom, but the Sweat Lodge that held me for days and nights as I looked into the void seeking any form of a rational answer to how to fill in the job description of my own creation. I suddenly felt like the cruise director for the Titanic. Worse, I was knowing that I also had to admit, that I may know every song and ritual of the process, but have no idea how to swim, OR WALK ON WATER. I had just been elevated to my highest level of Spiritual incompetence while the eyes of the world were upon me to do something clever. I was not feeling very clever. Tarwater shared my fear and both of us wondered whatever we were supposed to do with this sacred message.

The changes we experience, as a species from this point forward will be recorded as the most profound since the creation of this planet. We have seen it in the election of a new President of color and more than one nation in his lineage. It is a sign we have been waiting for, as well.

I would like to thank my friends and family who have endured my lifelong weirdness and dedication to preparing for this time. I send gratitude to the Grams; Edith Hendricks, Susan Cook, Mama Forsythe, Grace Spotted Eagle, Agnes Lone Wolf, Twyla Niche, Kitty, Cora Wounded Red Hair, Bertha Burch Grove, Mary Thunder, Ida, Edna Red Buffalo, Evelyn and Terry Eaton, Wind Daughter, Nicki Scully, Brooke Medicine Eagle, Barbara Vitale, Ms. Foge, Bella Abzug, Edwene Gaines, Star Wolf and all who have been active in my quest to receive this information. Gratitude to my life long support team of Brook and Alethea, Ravenwood, Bo Clark, Nancy Gire, Atma Kaur, Mz. Imani, Page Bryant, Scarlet Plume, Liisa, Ruby Falconer, Judith Corvin-Blackburn, Lulu Sliker, and Susun Weed, We are all blessed that Bruce Lipton and Gregg Braden have been validating the science that proves Shamanism to be a functional truth of our times. Most of all I would like to thank my partner, Tarwater and the many Grandfathers like my spiritual father, Wallace Black Elk, who tricked me into this time of being a Gram in my own right.

I would to thank you for hearing this call to action. It is those of you who dream and live the dreams that work the gateways of this portal of transformation. It is those of you who become the NEW-CLEAR energy of the new age that will be here to regenerate, restore and renew this planet who has just completed her menopause and is ready to emerge as the wise woman who will hold us for a thousand years of peace and prosperity.

WHAT IS IT YOU FEAR
  AS YOU ENTER THE HOUSE OF MIRRORS?

WHAT IS IT YOU DESIRE
  AS YOU REACH FOR REALMS EVEN HIGHER?

WHAT IS WRONG WHEN THE BEST IN THE WORLD
  DOES NOT FEED YOUR SOUL?

WHERE IS THE HOPE
  THAT FILLS THE HOLE?

IS IT TO RUN
  OR IS IT TO STAY?

WHAT DOES SPIRIT ASK TODAY?

WHY DID YOU DO SO MUCH
  AND STILL FEEL LOSS?

WHY DO YOU NOT FEEL VALID
  WITHOUT THE BURDEN OF THE CROSS?

WHEN DO YOU SEE THE LIGHT
  THAT SETS YOU FREE?

WHEN DO YOU KNOW
  THE GOLDEN AGE OF WEEEEEEE?

HOW WILL IT FEEL
  WHEN ALL IS ALIGNED?

ARE YOU WISE ENOUGH TO KNOW THE SIGNS?

JOURNEY ONE

Igniting the Blue Star Spirit

Together it is our intent to find the richness of Spirit the lives within each of us. We will journey through the only means this storyteller knows. We will connect through the truth of many stories as well as the one that connected us to the Spirit of Traditional Grandmothers that began a Blue Star Society several centuries ago. The codes of Transformation that they kept alive are the magical formula for surviving the current task of renewing and restoring every element and species of this planet. It is the code that carries us through 2012 and beyond.

There is an old adage:

The more you do, the more you want to do. The more you want to do, the more you get to do. Then one day you wake up and it is all doing you.

This workbook is intended to be interactive, because the Medicine is doing you and you are ready to set some boundaries and focus it's power into your vision and sacred intent. The workbook is designed to bring you into a support circle to give life to your own wholeness and feed the visions that you have spent a life-time dreaming. This is an offering of a series of maps to allow you to create and altar that will support your creation of spiritual practice as you carry it into the work and provide solutions. It is here to honor you as a gatekeeper of the Golden Age preparing the next generation to live in a new way.

This information is being shared as part of a ritual that began for me forty-four Solstices ago. Sharing it in this manner is a promise that I keep to myself. It is also a promise to the old ones who cared enough to pass on a few tricks of the trade of Shamanism as they etched my soul with their magical devotions.

AS YOU BEGIN THIS JOUNREY, GATHER A JOURNAL, A FAVORITE BOX OR SUITCASE TO FILL WITH THE MAGICAL TREASURES THAT WILL CREATE YOUR OWN ALTAR OF TRANSFORMATION. BE READY TO TAKE A MAGICAL JOUNREY OF CELPH DISCOVERY AND ALL THAT SHIFTING THAT YOU HAVE BEEN PRAYING FOR, CAN AND WILL HAPPEN NOW, IF YOU JOIN IN THE PROCESS, FULLY ENGAGED IN YOUR OWN GOAL OF INTENDING.

☪

The Blue Star Society offeres monthly classes and bridge

- calls bluestar times@me.com

YOU HAVE ALL OF THE MAGIC IN THE UNIVERSE SUPPORTING YOUR VISION. WHAT WOULD YOU LIKE TO BRING TO LIFE?

THE FIRST INKLINGS OF A NEW STAR IN THE SKY

It was a beautiful full moon night in 1972, as I nursed my baby daughter on a Santa Barbara beach. The fall season had been filled with many wonders while only two months before I had shared the aurora borealis with my precious one from the top of a Utah mountain peak. I had promised to show her the wonders of the universe, as she taught me the wonders of being an earth mother. These moments with this child in my arms were the most cherished in my life and have carried me through many a dark and lonely night in my more senior years. That particular night I was singing her our favorite lullaby about the mockingbird. I was making up new verses as I promised the moon and the stars and all of the love my heart could muster. We rocked and sang together for quite some time when I heard another voice chime in. It was clearly the echo of an older woman. She merged out of the shadows like an angel floating in from the waves. It had not even dawned on me that a young mom alone on a beach might be in any danger as I was feeling protected by my intent and my song. This angel showed up just in time to warn me of the drunken group of men heading my way and I gratefully accepted her offer to step over to her near-by cabin for a cup of tea. Her cabin just a few feet away from my own simple dwelling, where folks came to make retreat and take much- needed sabbaticals. Most of us rented these cabins from week to week. This old woman said she had booked the cabin for the holiday season while she worked on writing a new book. I was instantly intrigued.

That night I became friends with Eve, a radical writer and spiritual woman who had come to the beach to finish writing one of her many exceptional books. Eve became my confidant for the next few months. I was making some serious choices about becoming a single mother. Having no relatives in the area and no friends to speak of, Eve became someone to visit on my days off. My now grown daughter still has the angel doll that Eve made to put atop her very first Christmas tree. For three cherished months, Eve shared tea and stories of her very exciting life as a writer and radical thinker of our time. She was every young hippie's dream come true. As one who always sought mentors, I added her to my collection of inspiring women with the first sip of her magical herb tea. We had known some of the same Medicine Women and Medicine Men and even though I was only 21, we had been to many of the same places that she was writing about. She had a deep fascination for the Medicine Wheels in Wyoming. The Sacred sites were the topic of several of her books, and at the location of my family home. Her travels and writings took her all over the world and fantasy had taken me to join her. I was thrilled that she had found my own, seemingly boring home a place worth writing about with such passion.

Soon we discovered that I had taken art and writing classes from her old, friend Rupert Conrad. I had taken art from him in Wyoming while in High school. Her adventures in with the free thinkers of Greenwich Village and 'beat nick' cafes had been a place that both of these mentors had lived and writer or painted with great flair. She kept my attention for as many hours I could share with her. I cried more about saying good-bye to her as I left the beach house, than I did the man who had given me this beautiful daughter. I did not see her again for almost ten years.

The next time I ran into Eve, I too had won an award as a reporter. I had just left my leading position as an Associated Press reporter for Northern Wyoming and assistant manager of Chief Washakie TV. At that time I was barely old enough to drink, and was one of three women in television management in the world. When Eve and I spoke it was because I had my own television show; *Charla's Corner*. I was bringing in all of the controversial players in the challenge of strip mining, water rights, Native American rights along with and radical thoughts on the Vietnam war. Rupert Conrad and I had reunited and I was helping him write a book and set up a Native American/ Western History museum in Thermopolis, Wyoming. I had just given birth to my second daughter who had been named Dawn Star by the Grandmothers of the area. I had found 'home' while hanging out with old women who most thought to be crazy. Eve had dropped into the local nursing home to interview some of the old Grandmothers. One in particular had just helped save my life and that of my new baby daughter and our story, once again grew. Eve and I spent another month together as she finished yet another best selling book about the traditions of the old ones.

My own family had been on the Wind River since my Iroquoian ancestor Marshall Cook settled it along with his radical Irish wife, Susan Cook in the late 1800's. Great, Great Grandmother Susan's efforts to women's rights can be found at the historical society in Denver, Colorado. I was honestly living a seventh generation lineage and did not even know it! Yet it seemed that every Native Grandmother I met was quite aware of the Sacred Journey that was the blessing of my life. Each one pushed me to the next one. Every lesson became interconnected.

The day Eve showed up to be on my Television show, she had just accepted a leading role in a new Spiritual & Environmental (Spiritual ecology) movement with her good friend, Sun Bear. Both held a deep belief system that took the Spiritual Spiral path of growth and movement. Her book, THE SHAMAN AND THE MEDICINE WHEEL was about to be birthed into the world and her fame was soon to expand way beyond our little tea parties of the past. She was one of the first women of white/ mixed blood I ever saw with a Sacred Pipe in her hands to share with the people. Her story and collection of sisters of new thinkers, movers and shakers continued to grow. I was always quite delighted to cross paths with her, share a hug and sit with her in workshop as an avid fan and student of being a keeper of peaceful Medicine. Eve was a quiet guidepost in my life as I ducked and dodged the stricter Lakota, Arapahoe, and Shoshone Grams. She was playful with her message and always brought a smile to the movement.

By the time this wonderful woman went into the Spirit world, she had collected many Medicine bundles and magical tributes to her dedication to archiving the truths of the old ones. I was not present at her funeral, and knew that the greatest part of her that lived in me was her magical stories and a little doll that she dressed as an angel for my own little angel. I did not think much of her for another ten years, and seldom wondered who actually carried forward her Medicine bundles; always assuming most would have gone to her own lineage.

Life shifted forward. The summer of 1994, I found myself sharing a seat on the airplane with a beautiful woman named Terry. We were both teaching at an upcoming Medicine Wheel Gathering in New York. My husband was already there, having driven the truck of Sweat lodge supplies for the elders and our crafts to sell. I had been ill and my back was giving me a challenge, so the facilitators had blessed me with a plane ticket. Their only request was the to be sure to give Grandmother Terry a ride home when we returned to Atlanta the next week. Terry and I had a delightful conversation on the plane. We shared stories of mutual friends and healing circles we had visited. Terry spent most of the trip listening to my great adventures that had taken me from the reservations to the major media boardrooms of ABC, CBS, CNN and more. I was proudly showing off pictures of my two daughters and telling of the many adventures and challenges I was facing with them now as teens. We laughed about motherhood and she was assuring me that being a Grandmother was the very best, and I had much to look forward to in the future. She filled me with hope, and joy.

I wanted to attend her workshops, however mine were scheduled to happen at the same time as hers and we did not get to sit with one another again until our ride home. We giggled about how busy we had both been and how many old friends we had been able to play with during our gathering. It was as if we had known each other forever.

Realizing that our trip in-bound had been mostly about me, I opted to ask all about Terry on the way home. What a thrilling story of her life. She told of being the daughter of a royal father and a mother who was a famous writer. She shared about being raised by French Nuns in a convent. This was topped with the magic of her many adventures with her mother and her magical friends. We chattered non-stop all the way to her doorstep, and I asked for her phone number so we could stay in touch. I was half way home when it dawned on me that she was Eve's daughter! I gasped having had a dozen questions. Maybe now I would get to know some of the reasons that Eve had not taught about bleeding women as she lead shared the rituals that had been passed on to her. I rushed back home to call Terry to ask all of those questions right away. However, the conversation went like this on Terry's end;

"Wow, I was so glad to get to meet you. What a pleasure to actually have someone ask about me instead of my famous mother. I felt like you saw me, instead of just being her daughter. Thank you . I need to know that my Medicine is just as important as hers. I am so glad to have my own friend who is not just interested in asking me about Eve."

It took two years for me to carve out the right time to ask Terry a question not as much about Eve, as the Medicine practices that she passed on. Her methods of leading the Pipe Ceremony had been controversial to the traditional men and I was not sure why. Eve had always included bleeding women in her rituals. She had not banned women as the old Lakota men did. The men feared the counter clockwise energy of bleeding women and swore it made them sick and unable to bring the energy up. Eve had always included them in the mix, which was of great concern in public gatherings. When I approached Terry about her mother, she explained that because her mother was already a non-bleeding woman when she was given the Medicine initiations. It seems that Eve was not taught about how to do rituals of the bleeding woman or any of the taboos that many of us had experienced. Terry also explained to me that when her mother had wanted to pass on all of the bundles that she did not accept them, as she felt less than her mother. She did not feel she could be as amazing as her mother and had only claimed a few items. She let the rest go to other women students who were choosing to go through the same initiations that her mother had chosen.

Terry and I stayed friends until her crossing in 2008, just as I completed my initiation with one of the bundles that had been that of her mother Eve! It had come to me in a very magical way, and it was only after working with it for almost a year, did I clearly understand it's source.

Meanwhile, somewhere out in the ethers, Eve's Bundles were continuing to gather stories and take other women on sacred journeys. I had been connected to one particular bundle was connected to an ancient society of Blue Star Women. Suddenly, since the year 2000, a new generation of wild women were choosing to carry forward the bundles called **Truth of personal and planetary transformation**. This particular bundle had been passed on through several women and had landed in my hands as it's fifth keeper since Eve. It came after I had rejected it three times not knowing its purpose or meaning to me. It came through a third party with only a brief note of why it was being passed on to me and that others had left me instructions. She could not remember the name of the woman it started with, but she knew she had a tape of songs or something that went with it and she would get it to me year later. It took me six months of digging through mountains of ceremonial files that I had gathered through over thirty years of study, to find the Altar notes of the Blue Star. I was searching for find the clues that went with it. I had notes from the Peruvians on the Blue Star, more from the Shoshone and Navajo Grandmothers who had indulged me. I had pictures and words that had never formed a full picture until now as I put together a puzzle that pointed into the night sky for the answers. Among the many clues, I had found a tattered set of files from Grandmother Grace Spotted Eagle and Agnes Lone Wolf in my study material archives. This grease-trained envelope had my name scribbled along with the series of their old class notes. Inside were many journals and the minutes of the Blue Star Society. These women had gathered in the 1940's and 50's to rewrite the laws that affected all of the Native Families forced into boarding schools as well as to restore the FREEDOM OF RELIGION ACT. I had brought all of these women to my TV show and they had kept the notes of the information they tried to share with me in my much younger years. Never once had they mentioned the society until I was in my thirties. Since one was only allowed to participate after becoming a Grandmother, I had not attended a formal gathering with these women. Most were now in the spirit world. These women were quiet power-houses who took their magic to Washington to make change. The first version was what they prepared to go to Congress in 1947. There were in their own material, notes including the many forms of Sweat Lodge Altars, Ceremonial dances and family recipes for healing potions that both women had deemed important to pass on. The pages ranged from healing soups to the process of connecting particular ceremonial tools to create a wide variety of energies. I felt like I had just discovered the Holy Grail of the Medicine world. After searching the historical archives of three reservations of my youth, I found something that had been waiting for me all along. It was connected back to my own lineage who had settled the Wind River Reservation in the 1800's after coming over from Ireland and Germany.

THIS BUNDLE IS FOR WOMEN WHO ARE OF THE AGE OF 56 OR OLDER. ONE WHO HAS NOT BLED FOR AT LEAST FOUR YEARS AND IS WILLING TO STEP INTO THE CENTER OF HER TRUTH. SHE IS ASKED TO CARRY THIS BUNDLE THROUGH AT LEAST 13 CYCLES OF THE MOON AND DURING THAT TIME SHE IS TO GO TO THE FOUR DIRECTIONS TO FIND THE TRUTH OF HER POWER AND HER CONTRACT WITH THE OLD ONES TO CARRY THE MEDICINE WORK FORWARD. IN 13 MOONS SHE IS TO DO THE FOLLOWING:

*Create a six-pointed star with open space to tell a story. Make a connection with, to each of your master teachers in the appropriate point of the star. In this journey you will find your own power as you sit in the *center of that Blue Star. (There were scribbled images of samples of past women's perspective of what the journey of empowerment had brought them.)*

- Do two High Rituals with preparation and initiation to each of point of the Star. Maintain a focus on Wichapi the Dawn Star and what she is telling you to do. She is most alive between 3am – 6am.
- Do two of Earth (This can include Lodges, Working with the Plant Medicines, or the highest rituals of Her lineage as it relates to Earth magic.)
- Do two of the Air (This can include breath work, song, and dancing high initiation)
- You will do two rituals connected to the Fire (You may choose from Fire walking, Fire Dancing, working through rage and reconnecting to passion, etc.)
- You will do two to the Waters and within the waters. (You may choose from rituals of cleansing, plunging, transforming the waters.)
- You will do two major rituals to the Thunders and Two to the Stars. These rituals will come from new places that connect to your ancient lineage and special Medicine knowing.
- You will make a special bundle and carry it into activation of others around you, upon completion of the sacred journey of discovering the depths of Celph.
- The final ritual is a Quest to connect to all of the allies that will carry you home to your Celph. When you are complete and has found your seat on the Star Council, the bundle gets moved forward to the next SIS-Star.
- You are to journal the story and keep it moving with the bundle. Tell of your challenges and initiations. Make note of what new tools gathered along the way to carry the magic of this journey forward as your create your own magical, medicine bundle. In this journey you will have found all new connections and in that time will have peeled away all that is not true or does not serve the higher good. You will dance with shadows and light like no other time in your life.
- Each Sis-star in this circle will be offered a Council Seat should she choose to carry the work forward. She will then make a new personal bundle that is a Pipe (Cannunpa) of her own symbols and power that she has received in that journey. She will tell the story she experienced of the weaving of the Nations and the trust she found in Sacred Sis-starhood.

- There is a special ritual, colors, symbols and songs that have been carried forward by each woman who has been selected to be part of this Council. These rituals have been passed through time for nearly two thousand years. The rituals have grown and been molded as the planet and peoples have evolved. Your place in this council is merely a re-membering of Council Circles that welcomed your soul in the past. Your re-membering will be a connection to the contract of Spirit that brought you here to sit with the ancients ones in this place and time in your personal evolution.
- This Council meets in the cycles of the moon and seasons with specific instructions that will come for those rituals. You will be assigned a "Watcher of the Elder Grams. She will guide your hand until she returns to the Spirit World. You will then be provided with a means to connect to the Source of the Council, as well as to find the other men and women who have been coded to re-connect at this time of personal and planetary transformation.

THE ASPECTS THAT YOU WILL SEEK IN THIS JOURNEY ARE:

WHO ARE YOUR ALLIES OF EARTH, WATER, FIRE, AIR, THE THUNDERS, THE STARS AND YOUR SPIRIT?

WHAT ARE THE ASPECTS OF BRAVERY THAT WILL CARRY YOU TO YOUR GRANDMOTHER YEARS AND BEYOND?

WHAT LESSONS ARE THOSE OF YOUR FORTITUDE DO YOU CARRY TO THE YOUNG ONES THROUGH THIS PORTAL OF TRANSFORMATION?

WHAT IS THE GENEROSITY OF SPIRIT?

WHAT IS YOUR GREATEST WISDOM?

HOW HAVE YOU COME TO KNOW AND ARE ABLE TO PASS ON:

RESPECT

COMPASSION

HONESTY

PRAYER

INTEGRITY

HUMILITY

WISDOM

ARE YOU WILLING TO HONOR THE GOD THAT IT YOURSELF TOTALLY?

I knew I must go on this special journey, and it was, after all my 56th year A gift that I had rejected several times, was now going to take me on the ride of a lifetime. I knew this without even knowing the depth of the challenge I had just accepted. I took it home and slept with it for six months before I opened it. I read, I prayed and I searched. It seemed overwhelming to the touch as I fingered the brain-tanned leather that housed seven smaller bags. This Cannunpa Wakan of the Grandmothers who had hidden it for over one hundred years while it was deemed illegal to keep in one's home. Now it rested in my arms, and I was more than a bit humbled by the responsibility I was feeling.

It scared me so much that I bathed in sea salt a dozen times and prepared a full room to receive it. I even got a full physical, because I heard that every woman who carried it before met a traumatic death. I was not sure what I was supposed to do with something called THE BLUE STAR BUNDLE OF TRUTH AND TRANSFORMATION. I prayed all the more as I opened the envelope that had a note scribbled that said; DO NOT OPEN UNTIL YOU ARE 56 AND ONLY IF THERE IS NUCLEAR TESTING AND WAR GOING ON IN THE WORLD.

Many of these old women who had written this had been anti-war activists, and keepers of Crazy Horse's Nuclear Medicine prophecy. They had not been lightweight women, in any sense of the word. The circle included many women I had known in my life. It was not until now that I realized they had all known and worked with each other in the past. My coming to be carried by this bundle had been set into action many years before, yet it would take me months to figure that out. Grandma Grace had always called me Epiphany's Thunder Child. The date of my birth was one of the first atomic tests on the planet. My first breath on earth was of BLUE atomic fallout, and my life had indeed been filled with epiphanies. Reclaiming this treasure , not as a curse of poor health , but a means of accessing higher frequencies of transformation was the biggest of all. Grace and I had known each other since my TV show in Thermopolis, where she had been a regular participant. She had been known for her work as an activist as much as for her role as the wife of Wallace Black Elk. I had worked with both of them until they left this world, and their teachings will be etched in my soul forever more.

This particular journey of thirteen moons that would follow would be my shattering and rebirth unto this planet and the sacred task that I had contracted for long before that first breath. This was the tool of transformation that would give birth to my soul as a Sacred Grandmother of a New Golden Age. It was not until I had slept with this bundle for the six months that I was ever made privy to the fact that it's journey had started with my old friend Eve. Only in this moment did I clearly understand the magic of right timing as we dance around the spiral which always takes us back to the crossing points of meeting ourselves over and over again. This bundle did not come to me as an accident, yet a sacred intent that had been set into motion, the day I took my first breath on this planet. This moment was what all of the past episodes of life drama had prepared me to step up and BECOME ME, as sacred woman of the stars.

THE JOURNEY TO FIND THE SOUL OF CHARLA JO PUMPKIN....

This assignment seemed filled with glamour and endless possibility. I began it like all past sacred assignments with full engagement in the process. I had slept with that bundle from Summer Solstice to Winter Solstice and had begun reading everything I could about the Blue Star energy. I was suddenly and finding women all over the world who carried the same energy or some form of Star prophesy. Wind Daughter, now of the Panther Lodge carries a vision of the Beta Star bundle. Page Bryant had just written a book about the Star walking with the Gods of Egypt. Though I had known and worked with many of the Elder women of the Medicine ways, it was only now that I was recognizing the Star aspects of our mutual relationships. One woman led to another. The questions began, and within the first week of my seeking I was carried to North Carolina to sit with Grandmother Barbara Blue Star Vitale.

This Grandmother was in a health challenge and had called me to sit with her. It was a deep honor to share with one of the very first white women of our generations to Sun Dance in Pine Ridge and Rose Bud, South Dakota. She shared Elders with me who had been a huge part of my own story. Though we had known each other for years, this was the first time I sat in her home and shared her own Sacred Story. We had both been honored as members of Gram Twyla Niche's Peace Elders Council. We had sat in sacred council many times, yet never had a one on one until that day. We laughed about how we had passed each other in South Dakota over and over. We had endured fire ants and floods in Texas and puppy soup at far away feasts, yet it was this Blue Star bundle that called us to sit together with the tea cup and journal for the next series of lessons.

My Earth Father was born in Rapid City South Dakota. When I was a child he and my mother would threaten to give me back to the Indians if I did not straighten up. Guess I must have been quite a challenge, as I found one of my great soul journeys at the side of a famed Lakota Medicine Man also from South Dakota. It was no accident that I had begun Sun Dancing there in 1990. My own ancestors had danced with the same Lakota families over one hundred years before. Those pioneers of my lineage began settling the reservations of Wind River and Golden Colorado. Through out my life, I had traveled back and forth through those Black Hills a hundred times and now I would Dance them into my soul. When I got there, everyone had assumed I was Grandma Blue Star's daughter. Maybe it as our red hair, or maybe it was our energy. Whatever it was, I had walked in this fine woman's shadow on more than one occasion, and now I would come to understand the reasons for that part of my spiritual journey.

The contents of the envelope about the Blue Star energy had been sourced to a circle of Grandmothers who had come together to activate the codes during the great depression into the 50's 60's and 70's. All of these women had been Sun Dancers and activists. They had written all of the foundation material for the FREEDOM OF RELIGION ACT as it was passed in 1947 and again in 1978. They had been behind every treaty that involved freedom of the Native families. These tiny women dressed in calico were a huge brain trust of all nations. They had learned to read and write under the punishment of the nuns and priests. Finding women of other tribes who also carried the code of transformation, they joined hands. They made it to Washington wearing their simple frocks, carrying grease stained bags of notes. They would use this tool of the white man's language of power to regain their language, songs and keep traditions alive. Many had thought these ancient ways to be lost. Yet these quiet old women had kept it all alive. They had come up with their own code talk and a means to keep the magical healing formulas and rituals intact. They were quiet on one hand and well spoken on another. They were the voices of protest behind atomic and nuclear bombs. They were the voice of freedom that walked side by side with Martin Luther King, and the masters of transformation. They were the first nations on this planet. Even in death, these women, who had thought to be silent, had spoken a voice in the ethers that had created the most amazing shifts in consciousness on the planet. History does not record them, no one knew but their own tribe, and families what they had done. They left this world without ever standing up to take a bow for their courage. They left here having stitched together consciousness within the fiber of the Great Star Quilt that blankets the world with spirit of hope, help and happiness.

The concept of the wisdom had been kept alive in the essence of the ceremony. These old tools maintained the inner frequencies of the planet. These old women left behind a formula that they deemed important enough to pack away in sage lined suitcases, shared by mice, dust and mold. The messages ranged from healing soup recipes to government reports that allowed them to understand how to change the restricting laws. They were filled with as many questions as answers. For me they brought an entire shift in my being that continues everyday as I step into the center of my own Star.

At the point where I finally felt ready to sit with the tattered notes, I found it all quite daunting. I had spent three years cleaning old storage lockers that some of these ladies had left behind. I had cleaned trunks in broken down vehicles on four reservations that had become vaults of time. I had gone through every form of doubt and distrust of the source. I cleaned and cleared under the constant pressure of the Grace's beloved husband. He had promised her that no one would go through her underwear, yet her most important messages had been buried in those old clothes. The old one made me do all kinds of ritual to earn the right to clean out these boxes and suitcases filled with magazines and memories. These old women had many friends and between them they maintained well-organized files with names and pictures of every young women, reporter, activist and potential fundraiser or support system that might help them reach the goal off FREEDOM for an enslaved nation. They had been the coyotes hiding behind the simple ways. All the while they created some of the biggest transformation in the history of this nation. They had lived in Wyoming, Colorado, South Dakota, Nevada, New Mexico, Arizona and Oklahoma. They had lived simple lives and most of them had been school -teachers at some point in their lives. All of them had known the punishment of boarding schools and loss of family lineage. All of them had found their power in the silence that became a voice of change.

Knowing that I must first take this set of instructions along with the Medicine bundle to Vision Quest for four days and nights was imperative. It was one of the only ways I knew to validate all that was seeping into my brain in dreams each night. I had just come out of three years of very intense one –on- one Medicine training as the completion of a twenty-eight year commitment to this old Medicine Man. It had been over the top amazing. It had been brutal hard and even when he held me to tell me I had exceeded his greatest expectations; there was something missing of being a woman. He could tell me what Grandma would have done, but he was not a woman. As I researched this Blue Star, there was much he could never have spoken. I would only be able to hear it, when I had learned to access the portals of the Grandmothers, not his. I could never have learned it from them just telling me what to do, I would have to go out and do it for myself. Now I had a road map, a Star map to follow, and I knew this to be a tremendous blessing and honor as a gift for all of the years I hung in there.

One of my great sorrows was how much of the material was stolen as we read it and worked the magical energy. We went back and forth in ritual for over three years and each time we went back to the house, more of it had disappeared. The four of us who did the work only the memories of the rituals with Grandpa to verify what it meant or how it was used. We recorded endless hours of tape that now reside somewhere with a disgruntled family member or someone who lifted it from his altar for ego purpose. It does not matter. For me, the knowing is inside my heart, as it should be. I don't need the three storage lockers of notes and ceremonial tools to know the truth of working the process with integrity and honorable intent. He intended it to be that way, as did the Grandmothers who knew the value of traveling light. So the endless days and nights of doing ceremony with the notes will forever live inside of me.

I am a Grandmother now, and I needed to access the information and find the code of my own Akashic contract within my own wise woman soul. By questing with this bundle the journey deepened. I knew I would gain as many new questions as I answered. I had deep gratitude for the amazement that unfolded to show me a movie of my own Spiritual life.

Every Winter Solstice since my twenties I have gone on a meditation vigil Spirit Quest into the longest night. Sometimes it has taken me to a lodge, and sometimes to a hotel room so I can shut out the world. Over the past twenty-one years, it has taken me to a portal of one form or another at my ceremonial home in Alabama, Hawkwind. This ancient ceremonial ground is over seventy acres of Altars. By now it takes two full days to clean all of the Altars of the land and within the house to gather the tools of transformation. It would take an 18-wheeler to carry the stacks of magical tools that have come to this home. One wonders what choosing that kind of BURDEN is all about? (It was no wonder my that shoulder hurt so badly!)

This specific Blue Star Initiation began 12-21-05 as I completed my final vow to my role as SAGAY to the Medicine Man. (This was his version of calling me The Sacred Staff you lean on, and beat some of the names I had been called in my corporate incarnation.) Having also just completed 32 major dental surgeries to rebuild my shattered jaw and mouth, I was finding a whole new voice. I had a new titanium jaw after years of intense grinding and shattering of the bones. I had been ill with infections off and on for three years. Every 21-28 days I went down even harder. No longer bleeding, my cycles continued, only now they were about poison flowing from my body, mind and Spirit. I was in serious pain and was seeking some pretty big answers. My anger at the dentist who had infected me was over the top. This high priced specialist had been sloppy in his work, had charged me nearly twenty thousand dollars and had left me with infections and more pain than I had taken to him. The only good part of the surgeries was that I had used each time under the sedation to journey to the ancestors. I had put on a head set with Chakra Music of Star Wolf, the healing journeys of Nicki Scully or songs of Mz. Imani. In every process I was comforted knowing that I had Sacred Sis-star with me. In this healing I formed a team and have never felt alone. The process of activating the transformation at a cellular level allowed me to begin to work on my entire body, organ, by organ and cell by cell. I did it on purpose, mindful that I was seeking a specific result and the ability to move in my work with a body that was whole and no longer managed by pain. I was seeking a new bus driver, and a new direction to drive the bus. I had big goals of building nurturing centers for children all over the planet. I had dreams of supporting a broader picture of planetary transformation. I was not thinking small, yet my body needed way more energy and clarity to meet this type of goal. Each time I went into surgery, I took this intent into my subconscious to search for all of the ways to give birth to my vision.

Meanwhile in my day-to-day life my relationships were all at question. The way old friends and family treated me felt like judgment. It seemed as if jealousy and envy were all around me because of my relationship with the old ones. I had been in the silent scream of pain with my jaw for over a year, and no one was noticing. I was clinging to every workshop and tool with whatever steam I could manage. I felt empty, alone at Hawkwind. I was embarrassed that in my brilliance, I knew nothing and only felt pain. I was so weak I barely got to see the grand kids. I felt my soul being held hostage. My Medicine partner, Tarwater was being challenged as well. His liver had given out, and we were doing everything we could to regenerate. The old support system was gone and now I watched Tarwater seeming to go one piece at a time. At the same time, my father, was shifting into his 80's. My male balance was not a balance at all. I knew it and had I no way of knowing how to self generate that balance. I begged, I cried, I expressed in every way, and still no one seemed listening to my prayers for help; AT LEAST ON THIS PLANE.

This emotion carried me to the Winter Solstice quest. Calling in my two main apprentices of magic and mystery, we did the annual clearing of the land. We walked to every Altar in the portal; beginning at the Peace Pole at the gateway. We would weed, clear and smudge. We took down old prayer flags and put up new ones. We even put some women's moon blood at the gateway to protect us and we moved into the land. We cleared the cobwebs at the Fairy house and made way for the little people to dance into the longest night. We hiked up the hill take us to the Women's Medicine Wheel and we move around it, CHILD, MAIDEN, MOTHER, CRONE. We cleared and smudged and walked further to the site of Stone Mesa Medicine Wheel that was in progress. Tarwater had declared that it will be his future burial grounds, and I feel all kinds of emotion about now being trapped at Hawkwind to care for his potential ashes. I was bond by the memories and visions of every Elder who blessed this land and left us a big stone to carry forward. I quaked at this portal and give it an extra big smudge. We put out new prayer flags and moved to the Dance grounds. We made a stop at each of twelve gardens. These small portals carry the Medicine blessings of every Elder who passed a bundle on to us. As always, I pause and beseech them to carry me on this journey. I ask them to guide my knowing as to how to carry my Spiritual life and guide those who come to Hawkwind for their own Spiritual growth. I know that I must now move beyond this gateway into other places, as well. I knew it was time to release the main caretaking of this place to others, yet my trust value and control issues were standing in my way.

On this day we paused and changed the flags of many Altars. We cleared the big Spirit houses to the moon and the sun. We took time to have a snack and a drink of the healing waters. And then we moved forward around the circle to WOBI'S Circle, where we hold and all night Soul Fire each year. Wobi was my best pal dog that got me through my last major bout of illness. The Coyotes got him and he died in this circle. It is a special place that we have always known to be a major source of Spirit allies who have always resided on this land. I made special honor to all of the dogs who have kept us alive and smiling.

The next portal is the Sweat lodges. We have three to honor. Today, new prayer flags replace last year's energy. We stop and honor the many sweat lodges of the past year and the completion of my own focus on working with the Thunders We make sure all of the blankets, sheets and lodge supplies are in order. We clean the teaching arbor before we hike to the Moon Lodge. This Sacred Women's place was the second structure we put up over 20 years ago.

I don't take care of the moon lodge any longer. I quit bleeding when I was in my 50th year. I celebrated with a wonderful initiation lead by Nicki Scully . On this particular Solstice, I allow the apprentice clear the Altars, while I wrote a note to the younger women in the worn out journal. Another smudging of sweet grass and together, we move around the portal of circles to clear the family camp, the garden, the shower house, bunk- house and on to the Road Kill Café and Disco. We pass through the trading post and prepare the car for the bigger trip.

By now it is dusk. One of us drives with sage smudge in the front seat. Sister in the back seat has a broom to sweep the energy and a renewal of cedar smudge. We pass all of our neighbors and circle the town. We work the back road behind Hawkwind and giggle as the corn meal flies in our faces. We place new prayer flags at all the corners of the four directions of the land and we pray forward. It is exhausting, yet feels like the kindest way to honor the land that works so hard to support the visitors who come through each year. It is also a great source of giggles and humor as we watch ourselves play out the role of the town's crazy women.

I have filled many a fine journal with all that the energy of this land has taught me. It certainly was the proper way to prepare to move into this **Blue Star Bundle of Truth and Transformation**.

The next day I begin to clear all of the Altars in the house and the Healing room. I wipe down the pictures and gather all that is no longer needed on each Altar. (At this time each year I honor a new intending of my own ceremonial work from year to year, the tools of transformation seem to evolve.) I clean and clear each ceremonial tool with sea salt and smudge and gather them for my journey of the longest night. I prepare the lodge and ceremony room to receive me. Then I am ready to begin a cleansing fast. It is time to pray and journal into the next season that begins my Sacred New Year. I will review what I learned from the past year's intent and what I choose to carry forward into the next year. I gather all of the ceremonial clothing and jewelry. I select, which is to be passed on to the next apprentice, and what I will continue to use in my magic work. It is a sorting time and one of major new beginnings.

This takes all day and the Ceremony room is filling with bags, boxes and crazy vessels of intent. (NOTE: that I use the word intent, rather than intension. I feel there is no reason to ever add tension to the desires of the soul. Thus each I write a new intending that goes something like;

I Charla accept the understanding, compassion, wisdom and responsibility of peace, healing and a safe container of abundance that come from the unlimited universe that allows me to work with the element _____ and to develop the Medicine to serve the vision of_____. I promise to use this work wisely as honors the visions of the old ones that keep the young ones alive.

I am restless and do not want to stop until the task is complete. Thus the Ceremony room is where I land for the next two days and nights. I cleanse with a Sacred Stone People's Lodge some place in between. I sit and pray with Cannunpa Wakan and cry for all of the sorrow and fear of the coming Earth Changes that I am feeling. I pray all day and into the night. I have done this same process a couple times a year since I was a teen. However, in this Crone time of my life, I feel the importance of the process seems clearly one of the biggest shifts ever.

It is within the longest night that I finally opened *the* BUNDLE and envelope with my name. I sobbed as I read the instructions, which I have chosen as my guide for this bundle of TRUTH AND TRANSFORMATION. I hold my breath for hours as I gasp at the depth of the work ahead. This process was not for a weak hearted woman and would require some pretty intense negotiation to meet all of the aspects of the assignment. . Part of me is giddy at the challenge set before me, and the other part of me is frozen in space and time in complete disbelief that I have been chosen for this journey. Every issue of worthiness slapped me in the face. My sore jaw had still not healed from the abuse by a greedy dentist and it throbbed like arrows in my face and neck. My heart began to palpitate and I am had the worst anxiety attack I have had in months. (If I base this on how brutal the pain had been over the past 24 months, this is BIG STUFF!)

I decide the only way to manage the depth of the initiation is to set up the process in true Capricorn style. I placed five really nice new purple storage containers around me. I put a pretty sticker on each one to indicate; EARTH, WATER, FIRE, AIR, AND AKASHA. I put a blank journal in each one and began to sort the ritual tools by element or instruction given as I received it some where in the past forty plus years. Suddenly, I know that four days and nights simply will not cover this task. Rather than hit complete overwhelm, I begin to outline the prime notes in my memory bank. I write about each ceremony as best I can, until I am overwhelmed at how much stuff I have, and all of the amazing people who have found me worth sharing their magic. I write for endless hours and sing and sob. Then I pray hard and do it all over again. Clearly it will take all year to record this story even if I do not do anything but write about what is being wrapped up to put into these containers. I had no idea the depth of my experience until now, in this moment and time and why I am sitting in this Sacred Circle all alone with this bundle of TRUTH AND TRANSFORMATION. As I completed this particular longest night; I began the longest walk to the source of my soul!

Thank you Great Spirit for giving me this day
I thank you for the healing and help along the way
I thank you for my friends and hope and all my family
I thank you Great Spirit, for all that you give me.

Thank you Great Spirit for wisdom on this day for showing
me compassion, and granting courage for support
I thank you Great Spirit for compassion and rebirth
I thank you for another good day to walk upon this earth.

JOUNREY TWO

The Wake up call

A SINGLE THOUGHT CAN CHANGE YOUR LIFE! WAKE UP AND LIVE THE LIFE YOU LOVE...

Those were the words at the top of the page. Instructions were attached to many pages, each giving connections to the elements and the four directions of Native Source. There were ingredients to set up four kinds of Eagle Altar, based on the seasons and need for understanding. One Eagle would teach you to fly above the situation of life and to look at it from the perspective of space and time. While another Eagle Altar was to assign someone else better eyes to look back and see a disruptive situation with compassion. Still another Eagle was to be assigned the task of finding the way to safety in the storms. The final Eagle was assigned to help one find their way back to their Spirit home with new eyes, stronger wings to fly and a support system that wove into the Universe. Grandma had outlined ways to engage those Spirit Eagles into service and why any woman would want to call in fierce assistance in protecting her family and home. It did not matter if that woman was Native American, she was calling in the great eyes to see all of the options before making a solid choice that would effect the nest she had created for her family. Grandma gave songs and signets to engage the process, and then reminded that all of life was about perception of challenge or opportunity to create change. Everything in divine order, or as she said; " *Everything is just the way it is supposed to be. Where you stand and how you see that situation is the one that might need to be adjusted!*"

The instructions of connecting with the Eagle allies reminded me, if you want to change the world...START WITH YOURSELF. It always seems so much easier to fix other peoples stuff before I have to deal with my own. Darn, this was going to be a self-help journey, for sure. The instructions continued:

CULTIVATE SELF-DISCIPLINE

DEVELOP SELF CONFIDENCE

HANDLE DISAPPOINTMENT

SHUN OVER CONFIDENCE

ENJOY TEAM SPIRIT

LEARN GOOD SPORTSMANSHIP

CHERISH THE MEMORIES

Grandma's reminders continued. *You always get what you focus on, so focus on what you really want. Attend to your heart for your nourishment.*

I sat with this for long periods of time. I wondered how many ways I had short cut my own nourishment while staying busy attempting to feed others Spirit food. I mused at how many days and nights I had clutched my own gut unable to contain the food mixed with stress. Even in the times when I had thought to be taking care of business, had I missed something of my own wholeness?

See Failure as feedback. You always get a result…it is how you decide if you have the result intended that will make the mark of success.

Well that was a button pusher. Somehow I had decided that my own perception of failure outweighed every success I had experienced. How had I allowed myself to focus on the what went wrong parts of life, instead of the what went right part? I had more skills than that, yet there I was lost in the great abyss of expectations versus results. In this moment I knew it was MY expectation and MY PERCEPTION of the effect of the results. Oh sure, lots of people had told me that I am amazing. I knew it on the good days, yet it is in the moments of feeling like I had wasted God's time that I felt like a total blob of wasted space. If I had not saved the world, changed every child's life, then surely I was just not doing enough. ENOUGH, whew now there was the biggest word in the dictionary. When do any of us know when enough is…ENOUGH? We grew up hearing that the great American system tells us we should always want MORE??? So I pondered what is ENOUGH…for more than enough time.

That night I held that Grandmother bundle tight, and I prayed until I heard my own message from Spirit and managed to write it down between the tears of joy for the ability to simply hear the inner voices of my own soul to guide me.

THE KEY TO TRANSFORMATION IS YOU!

* Have courage to persevere

* Create the Power of You

* Change your path if you are not living your Journey

* Follow your bliss

* Be silent

* Live in the now

* Give back

BE CONSCIOUS CREATOR....

MAMA I AM LISTENING TO YOU NOW, BUT I RESIST.
MAMA I UNDERSTAND YOU NOW
AND I AM DELIRIOUS WITH SACRED CREATION.
MAMA I AM HERE PRAYING FOR THE WOMEN
AND EVERYONE IS HAPPY.

I write my emotions, and attempt to release my expectations of what this journey will look like on my list of things to do. The list is getting longer as I reach into the past to heal old trauma and give life to the vision that is growing inside of me.

After countless journeys and wanderings

Through forests, tunnels and blunderings

After many trials and experiments

We return home to discover & experience the tremendous Power within US and the

infinite symmetry in being us....Sydney Bhebe

WHAT DOES A TRANSFORMATION INTO WHOLENESS LOOK LIKE?

Well there was a deep question. Everyday I hear folks claiming to be looking for the right change and transformation of situations that are feeling filled with discomfort. Yet, none of us seems to have a grip on the reality of what real transformation feels like, until it is way over. Then we only seem to get it when others have come acknowledge some visible change in us. The validation process is more uncomfortable than the process of getting there. Even when we feel something different, we are not really sure that it took, until someone else notices it for us or with us.

The next level of the assignment made me look from the eyes of an Eagle at my own choices in tools for transformation. Throughout my life, it had almost always taken on the form of a chronic illness or new form of disease to grab my attention and call me to the action already demanded of me. I had a medical record that each doctor read in disbelief, as each one changed the diagnosis, based on how advanced the symptoms had grown to a new form of dis-ease. Holding this bundle was intended to bring me to wholeness and it did not make the choices set before me any easier. The bundle, did however function as a means to clearly look into the levels of my own body, mind and Spirit to see what needs my attention and the means to get to the shift in a balanced and comfortable manner.

I was feeling quite anxious preparing for this ritual quest. I looked at the past months where I had not been able to drive, or participate in the deep rituals of my past. The medications had taken over one realm and Spirit had taken over the other. I stood in night hanging on to the walls with white knuckles of hope. I was in prayer day and night as I cleared from Altar to Altar. I gathered memories and cosmic assignments and realized that I was too weak to do four days and nights in the lodge. The six women I had asked to hold space with me had disappeared, as if they had not been invited. I was down to two or three and they were not Crones. I knew they did not have the juice to hold me, and I was attempting not to feel short changed. I had never let any of them down. It was my manner to show -up for them, always when I say I will. Yet, they were all flaking and I was abandoned. I prayed and called my Elder Ute Gram. She told me she saw my solar plexus like an octopus with tentacles going in every direction and everyone was pulling. She saw the dark cord that was choking me, and it was attached to the most important men in my life. I knew this truth. I had seen it in the night, over and over. BUT, cutting those cords mean saying goodbye to many. I am loyal like a dog and did not know what to do. Yet, I do know what to do and set a plan into motion. I was looking for trusted support system that was not appearing with the strength and commitment that I thought I needed. I released expectations of any need for others and attempted to do the work alone.

I finally agreed to let a couple of young apprentices help me to create a portal of three Sacred Sisters in the Golden Pyramid. It is not what I had intended. But I knew it was what we could manage with my weakened state. Thus, that is how two young ones ended up at my side for the better part of the final four days of ritual of the 13 initiations that I had endured over 13 cycles of the moon.

This particular year at Hawkwind we have even more Altars had to be cleared. We once again circle the land only to discover that some time in the past six months developers had blocked off the cave. Then we found the South gateway to the end of our back road had a steel gate someone had installed without our knowing. We had parked to hike to our markers and a strange lady yelled at us for being on our own land. Much to our horror, we found The West Gate had a steel gate that leads through our land, as well. No one asked us about putting up any of this, and we had not been there for so long, we did not notice. On this day the only way in and out of sacred home is the North Gateway. I gasp at being further trapped within my own portal of healing.

I had prepared the Ceremony room and the Medicine to clear my system and begin the detox. I gathered all of the AMA medications and bundle them up to bury them. I am prepared to take the risk of doing this final ritual without the foreign toxins that were blocking my frequency and ruining my life. I had endured four years of antibiotics and pain -killers. I was ready and the fast and detox . In Lakota bacteria is called Toka. That also means doubt and fear. I knew my body was raging with the Toka, and it wasn't all about the infections from surgeries. I knew the depth of my doubt and fear about the prophecies and Earth Changes had consumed every fiber of my being, and I had to ceremony my way out of it.

The Quest to my own Truth and Transformation reaches into the Universe. I am willing to pray and reach beyond the ethers to hear the messages of my own truth, no matter how much the recognition of my own perception of failure and success might be thrown into my face. I had to do something big in order to see the ability to meet my vision head on and bring it into a new reality. So far, twenty- one years of major energy and blood giving effort had seemingly failed. I wanted to know the truth of my own journey and connection to my soul's purpose, at any cost.

WHAT IS YOUR WAKE UP CALL?

WHAT DO YOU NEED TO TRANSFORM IN YOUR LIFE TO KNOW WHOLENESS?

WHAT IS THE VISION THAT CALLS YOUR SOUL TO ACTION?

☪

JOURNEY THREE

Compassion in the Air

Grandma said to know your story you must know yourself To transform your story of pain and suffering, you must connect to the story of creation and nurturing

I began looking at myself through the eyes of my own lineage.

I am Charla Jo, I come from the Stars and I come of Vision to Vision for the seven generations yet to come.

I am Charla Jo, Daughter of Shirley & Chuck, some wild and crazy draft dodgers who ran away on a motor cycle to Sturgis, trying to make peace in the War. (My dad has always called me Pumpkin!)

I am Charla Jo, Granddaughter of Edith, Toot's, who ran away on horseback to marry the hottest Fiddler at the Wyoming Barn dance.

I am Charla Jo, Great Granddaughter of Ella Louisa, who ran away with the Casino owner Jo Jo during the Gold Rush, to homestead in Wyoming. She was Daughter of Wilamena Pauline who came of the lineage of the daughter of Mable, daughter of Minnie Lee, daughter of Susan, who was pushed a cart from Plymouth Rock. There, her uncle, Miles Standish had promised her a new world. At age 13, she was kidnapped by the Arapaho Indians and carried off to South Dakota and then was rescued by the Iroquoian Medicine Chief, Marshall Cook, who took her as his second wife.

She was daughter of Matilda who was banished from Shannon Ireland for being a Hedge Witch, she was daughter of Caroline, who was daughter of the lineage of Christine O'Rielly, a famed witch who kept the hops for the king of England at one time. Her lineage carries us back to the Tribe of Ephraim and the daughter known as Ishtar.

I am Charla Jo mother of Kristene Brook, and Alethea Dawn Star, Richard Jason, several step-sons, and countless foster ones a many who have called me mom, auntie and Gram.

I am the Storyteller of the Star Council of Grandmothers and keeper of legend and lore of the healing nations. I came into this world with an Atomic breath, along with the first test explosions on the reservations. I was called Epiphany's Thunder Child by the old ones and trained into a world of mystery and magic from the very beginning. I have spent my life wondering how to fit in on planet earth and much of it has been laced with physical pain, which has cause d me to live much of the time within my own world.

My lineage settled the Wind River Reservation in 1872, where my family has resided in some form, ever since. I have sought to know what that has meant in my karmic/ akashic contracts as I have been guided on an exceptional Spiritual Journey. The times that I have woven into the bigger world, my juice has been the source of many huge visions that have created things like Cable TV, Cellular Telephones and Voice Recognition systems. In my authentic world, I am a spinner of many soul-utions and magical adventures. I share with you here my role in the Council of Grandmothers as this journey has taken me around the Great Medicine Wheel to dance with each seat/stone and life choice. I stand now in the center of the universe, prepared to re-create this being, body, mind and Spirit.

AS I WRITE THIS IS IT IS MY 57TH YEAR ON THIS PLANET. IT IS MY SHAMANIC - SHATTERING TO TAKE ME TO THE DEPTHS OF MY SOUL TO EXPLORE ALL THAT I BELIEVE TO BE A TRUTH AND ALL THAT NO LONGER SERVES THIS MAGICAL VESSEL OF MY LIFE. IT IS MY RE-BIRTHING YEAR, AND I AM SCARED. EVERYONE TELLS ME I AM AWESOME AND I SEARCH TO SEEK MY AUTHENTIC SELF.

To the Peruvians I am known as LEBONAZE, she who travels between the worlds.

To the old Rainbows I am known as GOLDEN EAGLE WOMAN

To My old Commune I am known as STRAWBERRY

To the Media World I am known as HEAVY METAL THUNDER & CHAZ

To the Lakota Elder I am known as HEYHAKA- SAGAY UNCI, Gram who is the Sacred Staff you lean on

To my Rainbow Community I am known as HEYHAKA WANBLI, the wife who connects the heavens and earth and sees shadows in the night.

To my Star Clan I am known as UNCI WOLHOLIA WICHPTOE SKECA , which is the Worthy Blue Otter Grandmother.

To My New Voodoo Friends, I am "mutha-fuckin' coon ass holy woman who's got as much head as heart. (This one always makes me smile.)

In this moment I wanted to know who I was to me, and that brought up many deep and sorrowful questions about my life choices. I wanted to know what I bring to the picture of life and what is my purpose. I had felt the assignments of "carry this sacred Message forward" for so many years, I had lost track which message was even important, any more.

The first part of this assignment of connecting with my lineage was sweet. It certainly reminded me that I came by my wild woman instinct quite naturally. It also reminded me of the connection of cell clusters and that vision I had one time about being my own great granddaughter, and someday doing it again. Thus the purpose of continuing this sacred journey was to maintain a cellular imprint on my spiritual consciousness.

The next phase of the assignment, however, was so tough it took months to be able to complete the whole story. This was to tell my life story by illness, disease and trauma a list what was going on spiritually in personal evolution. It was time to go back and find key illness and what was going on in life that allowed the illness a hook in the cellular system that was now shattering. Every disease has a story. It did not just happen over night. It is the same with planetary disease. It us over one hundred years to create the mess we are having to clean up today. The process is the same be it for your body or your government. Detox is detox. Rewriting history is a must for all of us to survive during these Earth Changes.

THE HEALING SAGA

BODY *MIND* *SPIRIT*

Age

1

2

3

4

5

6

7 shift , what was biggest transformation

Age 8

9

10

11

12

13

14 shift, what was biggest transformation

Age 15

16

17

18

19

20

21 shift, what was biggest transformation

Age 22

23

24

25

26

27

28 shift, what was biggest transformation

Age 29

30

31

32

33

34

35 shift, what was biggest transformation

Age 36

37

38

39

40

41

42 shift, what was biggest transformation

Age 43

44

45

46

47

48

49 shift, what was biggest transformation

Age 50

51

52

53

54

56

57

58

Who are you and what is your magic and soul's purpose?

Over the next few months I prayed for days and nights, seeking the next clues as to why I was working this Blue Star energy. The ringing in my ears was getting louder, and sleep was non-existent for more than an hour at a time. I was so shaky that I burned my hand in the middle of the night while making calming tea. It was a bad burn and the next level of antibiotics had been issued to avoid further infection. I had cysts in my mouth and all over my thighs and behind. Yet, I kept hearing that this was an initiation and that I must look further than my fear. I kept hearing that I was not really sick with some weird infection, but that the infection was my own fears rising to the surface. I knew I had to deal with my own story, and not just medicate it away. I knew I had to rewrite my story and begin with a new body, because this one was just too tired to do the work that nagged my visions each night and day.

I looked for clues as I worked through the years of my own illness and Spiritual aspirations.

* *I came with a blue atomic breath*

* *Had fairy like creatures visit as long as I could remember*

* *There was some connection with rock hunting with my grandpa and the blue sapphire ring I made at age 12*

* *The visits with Isis throughout life are connected*

* *There is something that happens in May each year and bigger at 4 and 7 year marks of time that seems to take my body a new healing journey.*

* *This disease is evenly distributed throughout the elements of my system.*

* *Whatever is happening is encoded in my DNA it has a tone to it.*

* *I am going through IN-volution, so what do that mean to me?*

* *I have passed this way before in another time in space and recognize the sounds and effects, and the transformation code.*

* *Gram said look at the painted star if you are born on the 4th, 6th, 7th, or 9th. She promised a clue as to how to find the tone of wholenss.*

* *Perhaps it was the many layers of sexual and spiritual abuse that I had endured*

* *Watch Cycles of 13 and every 52 years she indicated a clue to do with with Mercury and Jupiter.*

Some of this is about genetically modified foods, and my reaction to them. I eat out too much.

This kind of meditating and journaling went on night after night. I was praying with all of my heart that I had not lost my mind somewhere in surgery and that I would be able to be functional with all of these rituals and tools any minute. I was ready to change my name and move into a tree house in Big Sur. All I knew was that the more I examined what might be causing my pain, the more pain I was feeling. It was as if I had moved into a bubble of consciousness of being introduced to myself one cell at a time. I was sitting at the helm of the complaint department and cells had lined up for miles to let me know how many ways they had been abused under my watch. I knew that I had to see this through or die, but I was getting pretty damn bored with myself.

I read Mary Thunder's 6 commandments:

* Do not build walls and learn to transcend them

* Live in the moment

* Take care of yourself first

* Drop the ego and be real

* All things are possible

* Maintain Universal flow of give and receive

I reworked my lists from the practical points of how I was born, Why was I born,? When I was born, and how I was allergic to food and had chronic pain from the beginning? In spite of the dire illness I had also had amazing remissions and had lived an incredible life filled with great adventures and blessings. There was some form of balance that was happening there, yet there was something very out of balance in the means that it took to get there. I knew I had to put an end to the suffering for myself as well as for all my relations. I knew I needed to find that balance from a deep inner place and everything would be just dandy, once again. I continued to work the work, with the commitment to find that trigger that has brought me beyond death a dozen times before.

I made a list of every violator and abuser in my life. It was a long list. I made another list of all I may have violated. It was a long list, as well.

Grandma told me to make or find a gift for every name on the list and every morning at dawn go out and do this ritual;

- *Take the name of the person you are praying for on a piece of folded paper.*

- *Take a gift for that person and place it on the earth.*

- *Take some cornmeal to make an offering to the Spirits to help you in forgiveness.*

- *Place the name and the gift on the earth and surround it with cornmeal.*

- *Face the East and give thanks for the understanding of why someone might violate you in that manner… OR why you may have violated another.*

- *Face the South and give thanks for compassion and the ability to transform the fires of anger to a productive place of healing and forming new passion for what will carry you to a new frequency of wholeness.*

- *Face the West and give gratitude for the ability to call in a healing team that your trauma and the violation be healed within the deepest cellular structure of all of life. Thus your healing IS part of the Earth's healing needed so much right now.*

- *Face the North and give gratitude for the ability to take responsibility for a meaningful life and make accountability for all that is out of balance. Don't give out of guilt and fail to receive out of lack of self worth!*

- *Touch the Earth and Tell the Mother how you would choose to walk upon her.*

- *Reach to the sky and give gratitude for new vision and New-Clear energy.*

- *Stand in the center and hold the moment. KNOW the moment of deep release and peace within the cells.*

- *Now take the gift and send it to that person. It can be anonymous, Or, it can go to a strange person in need if you do not know where to find them. It is the gesture of release that begins to take the transformation to each cell.*

Repeat this act until you feel clear. Repeat it again each time a new issue of letting go gets in your face.

THE STORY OF TRANSFORMING THE DIS-EASE

I had taken time to write about one of my journeys with disease that took place in the past 10 years. It was one while in one of those seven year cycles and I had gone down hard while working on the road. Yes, I had endured every ritual known to womankind, but it was more than that. After some serious negotiating with a Sun Dance friend of mine, who also happened to be a OBGYN surgeon I gained some very valuable knowledge about healing choices. I was preparing for the removal of my womanhood, when I dropped even further. As he and I explored the many options, all markers pointed to several forms of Cancer or Crohns. At some point as we looked at my lack of insurance and the cost of diagnostic protocols; he asked a very important question;

"If this is the worst case, then how will you chose to treat it.?

If you are choosing Alternative cure, then go there now and don't bother with any of the rest of this. You are sick and you know you are sick, now deal with the story that got you that way. Deal with the way you allow your body react to stress and perceived failure."

I began a serious protocol of acupuncture and herbs with a Shoulin Priest the next week. I wrote about all of the trauma and abuse that had ravaged my life, and once it was all over, I needed to look from those Eagle's eyes to see what good things had come from the process.

I took some time and wrote about all of the things that I had not been able to stomach through-our my life. I looked at cause and effect. I knew that I had to rewrite the story. My mother and I both explored the time and place of choice that my body had made to allow disease to become a way of live. We both found the same time in my body. Her memory was one of high fevers, measles, strep throat, whooping cough and a long list of ailments that transpired one right after the other. My memory was one of deep violation. The connection of the fevers was quite clear to me. The hooks that had endured years of driven success/stress factors were also quite clear to myself, and every member of my healing team.

GOOD THINGS THAT CAME FROM THAT JOURNEY

* *I looked at the crap I had put myself through.*

* *I forgave others for the crap they put me through.*

* *I began to take care of my body EVERY second of every day and I began to honor me.*

* *I found acupuncture, chiropractor and massage and Chinese teas.*

* *I found NEOT for my food allergies and Silva to calm my brain.*

* *I began to write and write and write to find a new voice.*

* *I began to make peace with my mother and my daughter at the same time.*

* *I began to make peace with me.*

* *I learned all of the meridians and healing lines of the Thunders.*

* *I made new relationship with the healing team that is lead by me.*

* *I found my own healing song and learned the value of my tools.*

* *I really began to understand the energy systems.*

* *I began to find trust and hope in a Tattoo shop… TRICKSTERS CAME FOR THIS ONE!!!!*

* *I found ways to work with herbs and muscle testing and become my own doctor AND a better doctor to others.*

* *I began to reconnect and allow myself to trust in friendship and began to feed my own Spirit.*

* *I began to dance Gratitude instead of dancing away the shame.*

* *I was able to pay for Hawkwind, establish my healing practice and begin to become a full time writer/teacher.*

* *Lived long enough to become a real Crone.*

* *I have blessed a half-dozen Grandchildren and nurtured a couple hundred other children in my pledge to transform the relationship of parents and children living in crisis.*

* *I received and ACCEPTED thousands of prayer ties from people who let me know they cared that I stay here.*

* *I continue to find and receive more comfort for my Body, Mind, and Spirit each day.*

The second major story in the next cycle of seven years as my mouth shattered and required over a dozen major surgeries to repair. The unexpected trauma triggered a lifetime of illness and trauma. It was a huge opportunity to take my own journey of wholeness even deeper.

Some of the triggers:

* *You are talking to hear your hat rattle*

* *Your mouth gets you in sooo much trouble*

* *Shut up.*

* *Having spent years as a sale person and marketing writer of falsehoods to make a living.*

* *Having what I have spoken reduced or analyzed into what I was sure was NOT my message to begin with*

* *Having my tone of voice constantly a point of comment, even when I am purposely trying to be perky*

* *Not feeling heard or honored for the message of truth I was asked to deliver.*

* *Having to be a bridge between people and emotions or the family spokesperson.*

* *Double standard/ Double talk. I needed to know what is an acceptable lie and what is a lie to be punished for and how I had held the lies in my body as an internal betrayal.*

* *Speaking a truth from an exhaled perspective to make a sale of a product…verses speaking a truth from a higher perspective to connect someone in ceremony at a level that has been my own personal experience …that they in turn cannot replicate, thus they feel my truth is not real, because it is not theirs…*

* Honoring the storyteller that began with Bible stories at age 5 or 6 in church...to school drama... to the radio station...to TV...to Women's movement leadership.....to Spiritual & Environmental leadership. to Eldership.

{SHE COULD SELL A HAIR PIN TO A BALD HEADED LADY....SHE CAN SHUCK AND JIVE WITH THE BEST OF THE OLD GUYS...SHE COULD TALK HER WAY OUT OF ANYTHING...}

* Biting off more than I could chew...but being expected to take on the responsibility as part of my job or elder role in my family.

* Holding back words in fear of judgment with a tightened jaw.

* Threats On my life for speaking the truth crimes or offenses to myself and others...AND HAVING NO ONE BELIEVE THAT I WAS IN DANGER OR WILLING TO PROTECT ME OR SUPPORT THE VOICE THAT OTHERS NEEDED TO HEAR....

* Shouting at my children in an abusive manner, and being shouted at in those same manners by more than I can count.

* My strong voice feared, not respected, any more than my soft and loving voice...I get confused.

* Being the lead singer for so many years...giving way to others, and then being disrespected for the beauty of the song I brought forward.

* Hanging on by my teeth, to a thread of hope.

* Always called teachers pet because I was obsessed with perfection seeking validation, and being beaten up for being teachers pet

* The physical and emotional slaps to my face…and on and on.

GOOD THINGS I HAVE DONE WITH MY MOUTH

* Taught speech therapy to mentally handicapped on Reservation.

* Taught kids to read as tutor from fourth grade.

* Spoke up for the under dog from day one.

* Sang for family performances.

* Sang healing songs as long as I could remember.

* Could make believe, and never lost that skill.

* Spoke out for women as an activist since 1969.

* Spoke out for children as an activist since 1968.

* Spoke up for the needs of my siblings and protected them.

* Taught others the value of a healing song.

* Spoke of love and relationship and truth and some heard.

* Sang and read sweet stories to my daughters.

* Carried on the healing stories of the old ones when their voice was gone.

* Kissed with passion.

* Dined with more passion and tasted the succulence of heaven.

* Have spoken and sung BLISS.

* Taken grand bites of life and savored every mouthful, rolling my tongue around the experience.

* Reported on TV the injustice of people and environment.

* Spoke honor to those who needed to hear it and spoke to them opening of forgiveness.

* Took up a voice to support a vision of truth for more than I can count.

* *Taken on more tasks than most to honor the love I have for my children and grandchildren and to provide for the generations to come.*

* *Enjoyed speaking with wisdom and controversy to spawn something more than ignorance and apathy.*

* *Told stories to the children to pass on to the next ones yet to come.*

* *Talked my walk and walked my talk with no shame.*

* *Spoke my truth, even when it was rejected or feared or thrown back at me, I stuck with my story and lived it.*

WHAT I NEED TO TRANSFORM TO FIND WHOLENESS

EARTH:

The minerals in my bones and teeth accept the new metal…gentle and firm steps all at once…embracing my own visions without fear.

WATER:

How I respond and flow with the new DNA and emotions of being a Crone……My need to sip the healing teas so that which is poison might be gently released.

FIRE:

Finding Healing in the Fire, no fear of the sick monster, but see the transformation of Hel. Embracing the aspects of igniting the Sacred ritual Fires became more important.

AIR:

Speaking in a new voice that allows the truth to be heard in a compassionate manner, still filled with power of delivery and call for action. I am feeling a return of the investment of the breath I gave to the breath I receive. Time to sing a new song of life…joy and laughter

SPIRIT:

Being allowed the freedom to only make TESTIMONY to my own truth and allowing that someone else will have to speak their own.

THIS IS WHOM AND WHAT NURTURES ME:

My mate

My children and grandchildren

Taking care of me

Financial security

My herbs and sweets that actually nurture and heal me as I embrace them honorably into my DNA

Wise investments of healing time

My critters

My "healing Kids" projects

The tools and the Altars

Girl friends that I can trust and laugh with

Family break through

Grand adventures

Dressing up and being A Goddess/ Priestess/ Healer

Quiet days walking on the land

Massage, Acupuncture. Chiropractic

Books stores and antique shops

Writing and being published to share my thoughts and insights with others

Seeing children safe and happy on the land

It was in this moment of dialoging with myself about what caused me pain, that I understood that throughout time, no matter what was going on in the world, how each one of us relates to and lives within that currant paradigm is one of the most important aspects of creating transformation.

If you want to predict the future, then help create it. We do even when we think we are not, so we may as well become conscious co-creators of our own new reality. And perhaps that brought me to the next level of clues about this illusive New-Clear Energy that the old ones kept talking about.

Nobody can teach or be taught truth. We must find it out for our self. Some truth is always brutal. This technique is not without stress, empowering, and impacts all aspects of your life. Wanting pushes back what we have. Want is lacking something, while we think we are deserving something else. This leads to suffering. "It is perfectly okay to have anything."

We must let go of what we want to receive what we need.

This is my place of the new day and understanding. I look to the East for the beginnings. The tools that started at birth are the tools of the rattle. The rattle that lives in this altar comes from many places. Gratitude is given to the elements that have created these harmonies. I selected from the rattles that connected to each element and animal of my own magical relationships. The rituals began in the East to connect with the winged and the element of air.

In the East we create our healing fans. Since so many feathers are illegal we change the colors to shape shift the feathers into what we need. Our main fan is the blue macaw. It is for healing energy from the universe. It is the aurora borealis

To the East is Cannunpa Wakan, The Sacred Peace Pipe. Having been trained in it's many uses for over 28 years, it has become the backbone of my own life, and I feel that this Blue Star bundle has come to carry me home to myself at the time I have most needed it.

The East is the home of the Eagle and the place where the Storyteller collects the breath of truth to carry forward. Air is communication and stories. Air is smudging, of unspoken words and filling the air with song. It is the flute and the wind instruments. It is LIFE! Air is the smoke we give to heavens, the sweetness we speak to a newborn baby. It is the one element we can't fast without.

If you could plan what to say as your final words, what would you say to the world?

I am wide awake and hearing the Grandmothers call with the owls in the night. I gather the Cannunpa and hike up the hill to the Medicine Wheel. I begin to pray and I know it is 3 in the morning. I am asking the Spirit Grandma's how to get with my own healing so I can do something more productive. (OOPS, WHAT ON EARTH COULD BE MORE PRODCUTIVE AND THAN GETTING MY SHIT TOGETHER RIGHT NOW?) In vision they show me is my Medicine journey as a well intended trip on the Titanic. I see my regal life at CNN sink to the basements with the Indian boys..." *Charla Jo, if you do not behave I will give you back to the Indians".* It was my mom's constant threat and there I was, I belonged to the Indians. We had conjured each other. Now as the Ship was sinking, I had to admit that I could not swim. I saw ten thousand people drowning and only a few life jackets. I did not feel worthy to ask for one. I thumb wrestled with myself until I could agree on several things. I was going to have to let go of most of the tools to swim to shore. My shoulders were not very strong and I could not carry dead weight of others who would not do the work, In my mind's eye, I saw a friend who gave me life jacket...another friend helped me on the life boat when my arms gave out. One of the Elders howled and made me look to the stars for direction. I was doing well as I prayed my way to the center of the Medicine Wheel.

"GET OFF THE CROSS WE NEED THE WOOD", was the voice of my friend Star Wolf. I blubbered, and agreed.

THEN, I heard a male giggle in the woods and saw two blue eyes of the old trickster gleaming at the South gate.. "YEP YOU ADMITTED YOU CAN'T SWIM, BIG DEAL. HOW ARE YOU GOING TO FEEL WHEN YOU HAVE TO ADMIT YOU CAN'T WALK ON WATER, EITHER?" It sounded like the voice of Brad Collins at Isis Cove.

I fell to the ground in full surrender. Though I am scared about the depth of my medical situation. I am still convinced that most of it stems from the Blue Star initiation and I am taking notes on every aspect of my life and healing. I have dished through every memory attempting to log everything that might be triggering this much pain. The first words that come are about:

BETRAYALS....

FEAR (mine of others, as well as theirs of me)

My skills as an ENABLER

My codependence top the old one's visions

The consciousness of LACK

My constant issue of UNWORHTYNESS

The need to live the GRATITUDE

This sucks. I am in pain and I want a magical formula that will fix it. I want to wake up one day without the pain or fear. I want, I want, I want.

And yet, I know that I am the one who must do the work and decide when I have done it right, No one else can do that for me. I am too cool and have too much training to go down this hard. Yet, here I am down as low as it goes. I am dragging ass, surrounded by years of training and magical tools that all just look at me, like I am the fool who said YES in the first place.

I can understand that this is a Shamanic initiation of every aspect of my being. Knowing it does not make it easies and it still sucks.

JOURNAL PAGE

WHERE DOES YOUR HEALING JOURNEY BEGIN?

WHAT IS YOUR HEALING STORY THAT YOU WISH TO TRANSFORM?

THE SOUNDS OF SILENCE

In the ancient traditions there was a time when one was punished by banishment or the silence of the community around them. If one had done wrong, no one spoke to them and walked away from them when they entered a room. The Grandmothers pulled the shawl over their face to speak the unspeakable rejection of behavior. There was much power in the void of silence. When banished to that place one is caused to find the many voices in the silence.

There is the silence that is thick and filled with ANGER. It is hot, musty and very uncomfortable. It hurts even more to hold it in. It is treated as if it were a treasure that others can only view but not touch or heal. It is selfish with purpose to punish another.

There is the silence of JOY that says you don't need to tell anyone how happy you are. Every one can tell. Your smile shows it, the light in your eyes tell its own story! You can see it in the bright colored clothes and in the room of masterful art.

There is the silence that is IGNORANCE. It is thin and veiled with unknowing. It is a silence that makes one want to slap another awake.

There is the silence of AWE. That is so huge and so full of color and light and it exceeds words. It just hangs on to the smile and the body that wants to dance. It is found the moment that you are overwhelmed by the movie star, the Guru or the idea that you are in the same room with majesty. It is found in your arms when you hold a newborn baby.

There is the silence that is APATHY, it says, you don't care. If you don't look or acknowledge, it goes away. It's the thing you find distasteful; the beggar, the puke on the street. It is found in apathy of politics of the human condition. It is knowing, but not caring.

There is a special silence that comes with CONSCIOUSNESS. IT says that you will not lend your voice to cheer on the bully. It says that you will not support a cause that goes against the respect of all living creatures, great and small.

There is the silence that is FRUSTRATION that is tangled in the emotion of not being able to find the right words to speak the need. It is twisted and painful. IT feels nervous, lost and alone. It feels backed up against the wall.

There is the silence that is THINKING, the one that comes with lots of energy and desire to create mindful solutions. It says you want to be sure of your information before you speak it. It has an edge of perfection to it and it is tireless in its desire to succeed.

There is the silence of FEAR. That is deep in the lack of ability to speak. It says you are afraid of being hurt or rejected. It is a huge white ball wanting to be filled with words and sits on the tip of the tongue waiting its moment to explode. It is a scream that is bigger than sound.

There is the silence of EMBARRASSMENT that says if you don't say anything, maybe no one will notice that you have shoes on that don't match and a booger hanging on your nose!! IT is a sound of attempted invisibility.

There is the sound of IMPATIENCE that comes with a tapping toe and a stern look. While the silence of PATIENCE comes with a deep breathe of knowing that things will simply happen when they happen and there is no reason to fidget…(you say as you fumble with your hands deep in your pockets of knowing!)

There is the silence that says SCREW YOU. It is tense and comes with a visible challenge. It is all about knowing and not caring. It is about marking a turf without any reason, other than the moment of perceived power. It comes with a disengaging look that cuts through the juggler vein of life.

There is the silence of COP OUT, which says nothing and becomes the lie. It is the silence that refuses to acknowledge another out of a need to be in control. It is a rude and self-centered silence. It is lonely.

There is the silence that is muddled in the moment of simply being TOO TIRED to think. Your mind has stopped and you are unable to form any meaningful words.

There is the silence of JUDGEMENT that is a painful knowing as others look your way and turn away as if appalled by your very existence.

There is the silence that comes as a simple NOD OF APPROVAL.

There is the OOPS, I FORGOT silence. It isn't on purpose, it accidently happens while time slips away.

There is the silence of SHOCK that comes in the unexpected moment. We open our mouth to speak and nothing comes out. It sucks inside us and rips deep into the soul.

There's the GUILTY silence that feels gooey and icky. It steps from one foot to another in awkward moments that seem to last for hours.

There is the silence of SADNESS that comes in low deep sighs of surrender and helplessness. It is blue and gray and moves downward with glances that hang on the shoulders that sag with the weight of the world.

There is the silence of HURT FEELINGS that shrugs away in unknowing what to say. You work to empty the vessel of pain.

There is the silence of LISTENING with deep respect and open mind. The eyes and heart are engaged in the wires of connection that are being woven.

There is a silence that is CLUELESS is looks and sounds like one great big DAH!!! It is someone standing on your toes while reaching to give you a hug because your eyes are filled with tears of pain!!!

There is the silence that comes in the VOID of the coma or death. No matter how far you reach you cannot find a sound or a breath that says life. It is the silence that says no more.

WHAT IS THE SILENCE THAT YOU EMBRACE TODAY??????

THE WORDS LISTEN AND SILENCE CONTAIN THE SAME LETTERS!!! Pay attention to that message and find the balance between the spoken words of power and the power of the silence.

I AM CHARLA AND THAT IS ENOUGH .

I AM CHARLA JO PUMPKIN, AND THAT IS EVEN MORE.

I CHOSE TO TRANSFORM MY SUFFERING INTO PRODUCTION SOLUTIONS

I SEEM TO BE COMPETING WITH MYSELF FOR WHAT I DEEM THE PROPER RECOGNITION...I have been thumb wrestling with self for far too long.

I RELEASE THE STRANDS OF GUILT AND SHAME OTHERS ATTACH TO ME, I RELEASE THEIR DRAMA, WITH MINE...Please.

It is my shout of liberty and I know that I am well on my way to rewriting the story of my life as a victim of pain. It does not matter that the doctors have told me that the pain is a condition of my body until I die. I know that in some odd way, I can control the story that triggers the pain. I am now ready to move forward as a woman of many experience of Shamanic Death, ready to regenerate each cell to come to life in wholeness. And so, I can make offerings to the East and give thanks for more understanding of myself as I have viewed my life through the eyes of the Eagle. There may be lots more to see, but I have seen enough to form some clues about how to take myself, and others beyond the fear, guilt and pain that is the Toka of our lives.

☾⋆

JOURNEY FOUR

Courage of the Heart

Though I had been blessed with endless year of mentors and ceremonial training. I was feeling rather empty when it came to knowing which page of the magical book of formula would set my free of the pain and sorrow I had been feeling. I reached into the aspects of every tool. I did the thirteen initiations and kissed all of my monsters on the nose. I had walked the fire, and sweat for endless hours. I had prayed and danced and quested. I had worked my fingers to the bone cooking every special recipe to perfection. I had supported the development of huge gatherings and processed more young people than most therapists I knew. Yet within all of that, there was some magical formula that was slipping between my fingers when it came to my own wholeness. Maybe I was just working at it too hard. Maybe it was right there and I was looking into the distance so far that I had missed it. Maybe, maybe, maybe, was all I could hear and I was getting quite bored with myself.

One of the great prides in my life is the ability to get things done. It is a gift that has carried me on many a fine adventure. As the first-born Capricorn child of a huge family, it was a serious survival skill. The skill to lead the troops into the trenches has been material for outrageous sagas in my life. Seldom do I attend a gathering or function where my skills are not called upon, even if it is just to organize the refrigerator or lay out the food. I have always honored that all ceremony, all creation of vision comes three phases; the preparation, the actual function of creation birthed, the completion or clean up. If someone asks me to show up, I am mindful that they need me for all three phases and schedule myself accordingly. It is one of the reasons that I am asked to return and am welcomed on many healing production crews.

Having said that, it is time to get to the wonders of ceremonial growing. Each year at Winter Solstice, as I set my intent for my Medicine Journey. I am mindful that the process is going to push some buttons to enable me to grow and to see life with new perspective. Having gone through all of the elements and allies at least four years each, it was time to move into the center of the Altar of coming to know self and stepping into the Crone's Medicine. I had pledged to make relationship with Akasha and opening up to lost places in the heart. The abundance of opportunities to my personal growth presented themselves with each cycle of the moon and many a challenging day in-between. Just as I would think I had figured it out, I would be body slammed with some weird confrontation over something seemingly mindless. This was happening within all of my closest relationships. The more I reached out, the more my hand was slapped and the more "stuff" came up to work through. About the tenth time (hey, it takes me a while!) I began to look in the mirror. I asked myself, what is this about for me, and why does it keep happening? My inner victim was alive and well. Hours of insightful questioning and attempting to figure out the difference between their stuff and mine, was just too mind-boggling. Which led me to write a letter to each one and ask them humbly for their help. I asked them to write for me what it was that I did, or said, or what behavior of mine had upset them. I was certain that it was my keen button pushing ability that made me hard to live with. I braced myself for the worst critique, and waited. It took most quite some time to pull up the courage to answer, fearing that I would be hurt, or worse, would hurt back for honesty. I was sure I had done a hundred things wrong, vile and offensive. I feared the worst, after being yelled at by my quietest friends. The day the answers came, it took all I had to smudge them and open them up to address my thoughts and behaviors.

As I read each answer I looked for a consistent thread of truth. Low and behold, I PROMISE, every one of them at some point used the exact same sentence in describing the complaint. Each told a different story of how this action made them feel, or disempowered them. It seems that within all of my efficient actions of being there to support all of the gatherings were the words I'VE GOT IT COVERED. No matter what was going on, when they wanted to jump in and contribute or shine for an Elder is was hard to compete with my consistent being on top of things. As the team leader, I was getting more credit for parts of the process they had performed. They felt left out and overshadowed. I heard almost a dozen stories of how someone felt slighted with my quick efficiency that left no room for him or her to grow. Each one had heard the sting of my words, " Don't worry, I've got it covered!" Imagine that.

Well this one had me stumped. I thought back through my life when mom had always admonished me that I was the oldest and must lead by example. I found myself seeing how many bosses had loved having me on staff because I always covered their behinds and kept them out of trouble. When Ted Turner asked for a project, and I said " Yes, Sir, I have that covered," he did not ask how, but was certainly going to hold me accountable for seeing that it got done. As did Grandpa Wallace, numerous Ceremonial Elders, teachers as well as many organization looking for support. I have been many things in my life, lazy is not one of them. When I say I will show up and work, I do. I hold no regrets in that arena. However, I had no idea that I was not allowing for others to shine and I was sucking up more than my fair share of the accolades I knew that the journey to finding my balance in this dance was going to make me work mighty hard to loosen up my well earned control issues. It is difficult to be at a gathering and watch someone struggle to manage a project that I can do in my sleep. So I had given no thought to how I might be stepping on someone else's magical moment to shine. What a big oops I felt in that moment.

The journey continued. Each month I developed a stronger insight about the issue and how I might want to walk with this and be more mindful of others around me. By November, I was just about to wrap myself around the understanding of the issue when I found myself at Nicki Scully's side at Isis Cove, a North Carolina Healing center. Star and Brad were teaching breath work while Nicki was working with a healing journey. Integrating the work began to really move the emotions through my chakras. I kept asking myself, " Why do they not hear my heart? Why do they hear my efficiency as a threat or a critique of how they perform the task? Why ?" Just as I got to the next why, I realized my energy was blocked right below my heart. My breath kept catching at the heart point and struggling to move upward into my throat...ummmmm. At that moment, my deep Inner Voice spoke a huge truth,

"Hey Lady, this stuff isn't moving, …. BECAUSE YOU'VE GOT IT COVERED!" Gasp, shock, emotion flowing, Kleenex received. Oh my gosh , this truth was way too close to home. Could it be? Could I have built so many shields around me, using my efficiency tool to keep me from having to engage my heart tool??? Now there was a pause clause in my life and one to seriously review. For a moment I stopped breathing as if knowing I had the shield and would allow it to move or transform.

The task became more clear, but the means to reach the goal of opening up my heart became my focus. Low and behold, all year children and young parents have surrounded me. The only tool that works for them is to open up my heart, thus I am getting the workout that Spirit was needing me to find my heart.

Well folks, just as I thought I had figured out how to uncover the heart and give up my control issues, several facilitators called and asked me to take over for someone who could not make it. They said that when they called around, everyone said "Hey, you can count on her to cover it, even if it means she has to work a double shift." Thus they were once again reaching to my I'VE GOT IT COVERED WORLD. I continue to feel the ways to allow myself the opportunity to share the covered ness of each place I go, and still maintain my fast efficiency. So now the big mirror for me, was the bossy woman at the last gathering, who would not let me get my job done!

Today I stand at the South gateway and giggle about how many contrary ways that Spirit can offer me to find the ways to connect to my heart and others that we might have it covered together, and uncovered to Spirit that we might grow forward as one Sacred family.

WE DO NOT SEE THINGS
            THE WAY THEY ARE....

WE SEE THINGS
            THE WAY WE ARE!!!

The next series of instructions on this Vision Quest all focused on what nurtures and feeds the heart and how we express that to others. The pages had reminders scribbled in between the many ways to set a Sacred Fire and to lead someone into the portals of their own hell and bring them back whole. I was certainly not as concerned about other's hell as much as my own in this moment. I read back over years of class notes from Nicki Scully and the Grandmothers who had indulged my constant questions. I was not sure I had really listened to the answers that were right there in front of my face. Grandmothers opened the window of my eyes and the doors to my Spirit. I choose not to sleep through the event of living, but to experience it even in the deepest dreams. I must look at the answers that lived in my heart today. Perhaps these women and a few men had etched those memories, but it was through my own experience that I would have them as support to engage my heart in the passion of seeing my visions through to reality.

The Grandmothers asked:

WHAT IS PERFECT LOVE?
WHAT IS PERFECT TRUST?

THE SHAMANIC MINISTER HAS ONLY THE HEART AS A DOCTRINE AND COVENIANT.

THE TRUE REVOLUTIONARY IS CHANGING FROM WITHIN AT A HEART LEVEL.

MOVING FROM A LANGUAGE FILLED WITH WOUNDS TO A LANGUAGE FILLED WITH WHOLENESS IS THE IMPERATIVE OF OUR TIMES.

WHEN THERE IS NO ONE LEFT IN LIFE TO LOVE BUT YOURSELF, YOU BETTER FIND SOME PASSION.

WE MUST ALL LOVE OUR CHOICES.

I HAVE ENOUGH LOVE . (I chanted this to myself over and over attempting to really feel it inside!)

I ALLOW LOVE TO FLOW THROUGH ME AND TO ME.
(I waited to feel that love.)

WHEN THE POWER OF LOVE, OVERPOWERS THE LOVE OF POWER, THE WORLD WILL KNOW PEACE....
                                    Jimi Hendrix

When we use our imagination properly it is our greatest friend and it goes beyond reason and is the only light that takes us everywhere....
                                    Swami Yogananda

As Bruce Lipton reminds us...nurture the nature of our own being in order to nurture the nature of the entire planet.

WE DREAM THIS WORLD INTO BEING, AND IT IS NOT AS MUCH WHAT WE DREAM UTIMATLEY IT IS HOW WE LIVE OUR DREAMS!

This stunning flash came as a reminder from Dennis Hopper on a credit card commercial, as I looked for my truth in every direction. I continued to read through the notes of the old women as they had shared all of the reasons they could change the way the laws had allocated a life of pain and suffering for their nation. Those same principles of personal clearing were a must for any real vision to take hold and change the world. I was coming to know that the only world I needed to change was the one that is called me. I wanted it to be easier than that. I wanted to fix everyone else and hope that they would accept me for my warts and my, sometimes poor behavior, which I excused because of my constant pain. I did not like the way this process looked, as I had to face myself in the mirror each day and ask all of the hard questions. The answers kept pointing back to my own choices and the challenges I called in to seemingly validate my hard work and constant dedication to looking good as one of the chosen saviors of the world. No codependence going on here, I tried to assure myself.

WHEN WOMEN MAKE PEACE WITH THEIR POWER...
THE MEN WILL FIND THEIR POWER   ...IN PEACE

This was the next entry of my journal as I processed through the places in my life that had been ego driven and the places that had been soul driven. Today I was seeking balance in the walk without the DRIVE to make it happen. It was all about doing it with the rhythm of the healthy heart. The work did not have to move too fast and needed to be paced like a good Sun Dance. Yet I had spent my life exploring the many ways of using the power of creation for things that had not always benefited the earth, much less my own sense of being.

Through out time, women have been the visionaries to access the magic and the medicine. It is through traveling the portals of Seasons and space and time that we all find our joy juice to meet in the center, between the veils to see what we must really see to get us through the times of extreme transformation.

Now the Grams asked me to:

Make a list of your hero's and sheros.

This really began to connect me to the power of the women around me and how incredibly blessed I had been to know and work with so many amazing women. Perhaps they see something in me that I am not seeing in myself. I pondered and wrote in my journal some more. And work on their next set of questions. All of this was to connect me to my passions and allow me to come to know my own tricksters of the South gateway of transformation.

WHAT IS YOUR SHOUT OF LIBERTY?
What is power... and who has it?????
Are you willing to reduce the physical body to enlarge the Spiritual body, and could you get small enough to shimmer through space and time?
Do you know all of the places you lost your soul and left pieces of yourself behind?
Can you treasure map the vision into reality?
What and whom does it take to see it to life?
Can you see this project to life in less than five years?

As I continue to pray and vision the Old Crone comes. She shows me how to clean each piece off as I gather it and put it back into my organs and into my cells.

"YOU MUST BECOME YOUR OWN SOVIERN NATION." SHE REMINDS ME. " PAY ATTENTION. TELL THE TRUTH. ASK FOR WHAT YOU NEED. TAKE RESPONSIBILITY FOR THE EXPERIENCE. KEEP YOUR AGREEMENTS."

She left and I woke up in a cold sweat and vomited through the night.

This Sacred place of passion comes to transform our anger and allow us move beyond our fears and supposed limitations. I was always told Protection is the first work here. Yet now I know that when we call up protection we are telling our cells they have something to fear. We are far better off by creating a safe container and assuring our cells that they are going to be just fine! Many Elders are mindful to wear a special belt while working on others, thus embracing the wholeness in the middle of their being at the source of energy, source of energy, and keeping themselves from getting into some one else's drama.

It is within the sacred fires that we release and renew. A fire pit is awakened to deliver a stack of old letters, prayer ties and painful memories. Flames of transformation and filled the caldron to stir this into the healing and wholeness. We release the painful memories that hold us back and light a candle of renewal.

The south fires are where we do our cord cutting. Fire is the flint blade that will be used as old ties are cleared and a place to open for new life will be made with the skills of a Shaman. That Healing fire can be found within all of our sacred stones, and when we heat them into the lodges we awaken their memories. When we wear them and place them on our altars we are calling upon their heart to merge with ours and bring us new strength. Fire is within the Green Healing Stones that come from the center of the earth. Our first star living is inside the mother.

Fire is our Red badge of Courage and all of the ways we earn it, over and over again.

Fire is what surges through us when we know that we are really alive. In this moment of working with this fire I was finding my heart and knowing that I am really alive. The instructions did a reality check as to where I was standing inside myself. I was looking at a never-ending stream of unconscious becoming awakened inside each cell of my body. The old women told me to go to the gathering place of my soul and begin to look at what I could see and feel inside of me.

The messages from these old women continued to remind me, it is not about where we live or what is in our home as much as how we make home inside.

The Sacred Fire holds Council at the gathering place of your soul....

What does this place look like?

How do you get there?

Who is there from the past that you know?

How are the boundaries defended?

What are the colors?

What does it smell like?

What does it sound like?

When you speak to the council, what is your truth?

TO CONNECT TO YOUR OVERSOUL...

* *Form a circle of six trusted allies, surround yourself with sweet grass, tobacco and cedar, making offerings all around the outside.*

* *Form a six-pointed star inside that circle with cornmeal.*

* *Make an inner circle of special stones and bring in all energies to the highest good.*

* *Create a new world beyond scarcity and move into the abundance of purpose in life, by writing your sacred intend and placing it in the center of the circle that you will sing to life.*

☪

WHAT IS THE SHAPE YOU ARE IN?

IN - SPIRED

IN-TEGRATED

IN PEACE

IN WHOLENESS

IN-POWERED

IN-GRATITUDE

IN-ABLED

IN ACCEPTANCE

IN LOVE

IN-JOYING

IN TOUCH

IN-CREDIBLE

JOURNEY FIVE

Creating a safe container for TRUTH beyond FEAR

It makes a great topic for a seminar, the need to transform fear. We all relate to the need to transform a thousand things that tremble inside our wee minds in the middle of the night. Fear is a major ingredient in a myriad of diseases that come from the stress, or so our medical world would have us believe. There is the nervous stomach that becomes the ulcer and moves into diverticulitis and, if you are really stressed and immune deprived, it can become Crohns. Or fibromyalgia. That is just the mid-section of the body. Lets remember that we have heart, liver, gall bladder, and a few other meaningful organs in-between. Lungs don't do well when we spend so much time holding our breath, not to mention how chaffed the thighs get when spending too much time with our panties in a knot. Then there are stress headaches, grinding teeth or shoulders that won't loosen even when the massage Goddess shows up every week! When fear moves into our bodies, it seems to be a very hard tenant to evict. We can know all about the fear, we can feel that it is all about fear, and we can even talk about how to transform the fear, *all the while giving it life!* Fear can feel like the heartburn you knew you would get, but simply had to eat that spicy food, in the moment, was just too irresistible to refuse.

All of these aliments would be a good reason to go through the process of transforming fear. Yet, we go through the rituals, the meditations, and the intense mental dialog and then low and behold, we have to enter the real world. That world is filled with the phones ringing off the hook, e-mails, web sites, bills that increase daily, television reports, newspapers, freeways filled with too many cars, and bosses that want more productivity for their investment. Oh yeah, then there is that Social Security issue. Like, we are all not stressing over our futures and the cost of living, right? It has been months since any of us has met a stress free person. Perhaps the family cat is the only one not feeling the stress of these critical times. Yet, somehow, maybe even the cat is faking it to make everyone feel better. Unless, of course the cat found the nip!

At any rate, we are all most certainly feeling the effects of stress from the Earth Mother.

Lets go back to the beginning of this story. Here we all are sucked into the stress mire, yet having tools of transformation all around us. We have Stone Peoples lodge to leek the stress out of the tops of our heads, like a pressure cooker that has boiled a few minutes too long. We have drums, rattles and songs to sing our energy up. We have a thousand tapes and CDs of meditation and visualization, along with dance vibrations to get us moving to renew and restore the Soul. We have yoga, Thai Chi, and integrated breath work. Yet, many of us wake up in the morning, wondering what to do to lighten up long enough to stride forward around the wheel of life. When we remember to use our tools, they work for us. We call our friends delighted with our remembering, as though it was a new discovery. We hang on to that moment, until the next stress creeps in to fill the void and allows us to once again focus on displeasure.

One Native Grandma says it is as easy as getting up and making your own bed before making someone else's. Then put the right foot forward and step into the day with faith and hope. Oh yeah, and it helps to wear comfortable shoes! All great advice, yet the cries of crisis seem so much more complicated than that. Those calls seem to get louder and come more frequently with each new transformational process. It seems that just as we get the business settled, the car breaks down. We have it fixed just in time to catch the septic system, or the dentist gets an unexpected visit. Be it our own stuff or that of some one we love, we are all facing a full platter to process each and every day. Joy becomes the in-the-moment thing that drives us and sustains us. When we pause to pray upon the multitude of situations is a full time job for one and all. One of my Spiritual Grandmas used to tell me to kiss my monster on the nose. She would encourage me to get eye to eye with my fears. It seemed that it would work, until I came in contact with a new fear that didn't even exist prior to that day. For instance, when I was young, I never feared losing a mate. I had no perspective. As I grow older, like everyone around me, I find myself wondering what it feels like when one partner goes first. I watch my parents who have been married forever, and wonder how Dad would manage without Mom's cooking. I wonder how Mom would get around without Dad holding her arm or how she would settle his lifetime of business dealings that only he understands. Those are simple questions. Not really filled with much fear as much as filled with curiosity about how things balance out. I do wonder if *they* fear losing each other. Do I fear that if I leave this planet first that no one will follow my instructions or how badly they will mess up my perfect plan of how things should be managed? After all, I spent an entire life developing the perfect plan for living...didn't I?

How on earth do we transform all of this, even in the best seminar? Oh sure, we have all had a great life. Most of us believe in some form of hereafter, or the next life chance stuff. We believe we knew each other before, and leave codes for each other to find ourselves in another life. Yet that inherent fear of losing someone we love seems big. Is it the fear of being alone or the fear of unfinished business that tweaks us in the dark of night? Is this kind of fear a simple acknowledgment of unfinished business or is it the knowing that all relationships change form at one time or another. Sometimes from physical to Spiritual and back again. Are we all making the best of relationships? Are we grasping at time to make things perfect to please some mythical vision of life without any fear at all? So, are these thoughts actual fear or a simple acknowledgment of reality of the actual act of transformation that comes when a person leaves their physical body. We must now relate to them as a form of Spirit. Isn't it more important for us to act will the full compassion and embrace the now instead of taking up brain space to wonder about the enviable things that I will get to deal with as a natural act of the cycles of life? Oh so many questions which all lead to answers of the heart.

The story of fear seems to go like this. Just as we have dealt with one issue; like fear of water transforms when we learn to swim. Then, another new issue jumps in our path to allow us another gulp and lap around the roller coaster ride of life. Fear critters nip at the safe places of the soul, and we stand in line to feed them. It seems like we should have a stress standard for balancing the checkbook verses waiting for the lab report on a biopsy. There is a difference between an honest concern for an ailing grandchild, and fearing something that may not even happen. Most fears live only within the realm of possibility and only forms in our minds. It isn't like fear needs to be created, yet we do it all of the time. There is abundance for each of us to grab at and muse through. It is as there is a tree ripe with fruit, just dangling for each of us to harvest. Each fruit has a sweetness or bitterness to offer. Only after we have picked it and put it to our lips do we really know what we will savor. We watch our neighbor pick from the same tree and experience the flavor in a completely different manner. Why is that? Then there are the days that the tree is barren, awaiting a new drama to kick in enough juice to take bud and bloom into a full-blown statement of life. Even if the last piece we picked was bitter, we tend to go back to try it again. There in lies our challenge. All of us have certain comfort zones that live within the fear fruit. Many times within the tears of screaming through the pain of bitterness tasted, we bring up enough adrenalin required to calm the troubled Spirit. It brings us to the old catch 22 of, how do I get calm without the need for the storm to fodder the stories that will be shared with younger ones in our old and older age.

Sun Bear used to remind us to WALK IN BALANCE. It seemed a simple statement when we were young. Now the perspective of what is real balance in life has certainly changed for each of us. We each hold new respect for the gentle walk, and work each day to transform our steps into less of a push forward. We attempt to flow gently into the day kind of steps. Hard to do when the demands grow with the visions for planetary healing. The imperative is not to rush the process of renewal and restoration. We need to tend to it, to nurture it and then to weed gently through the new gardens of life. We harvest the joy that we have planted in our soul. We share that harvest with all of our relations and within that harvest comes another piece of PEACE.

It seemed there should be some cosmic answer as to how to pluck fear from the tree and swallow without any sorrow, grief, frustration, or remorse. There must be some ritual that can take us from pure panic to a place of personal inner calm. Is it the one where we go for a walk and sing a song? Maybe the song starts out strident and slows into a lullaby. Is it in the moment we simply stop everything we are doing and breathe and feel what is really happening. We gather the energy all around us and allow ourselves the overwhelming moment that comes back into focus of the one thing that we can do right to transform the present situation. The old ones used to tell us there is no problem that cannot be prayed through in less than six minutes. Some days it feels like that trouble tree just drops fruit right on our heads so fast that we can't even process it all for winter storage. We pray on it, cry on it, cook it in the lodge. We can do all of the ancient rituals we have been taught. Yet each of us has to admit that on any given day we are honestly holding something of fear in our lives. If we sat and made a list of every little thing we should be worrying about we would get nothing else done. So how about making a list of all of the things we do not fear ? We can make a list of solutions and joyful opportunities that can be even longer than the list of fears. When we live in fear, we are not living. We are perhaps, existing from moment to moment. We are limiting the possibilities of that potential joy that is waiting just behind the curtain awaiting the opportunity to take a well-deserved bow.

Tools or no, fear is real. The emotions of 'what if ' have to be played out. There is power in putting things into perspective, not to amplify the situation, but to honor it with pure thought and insight. To acknowledge fear is to honor its power and give it due respect. To hide fear, is to push it down into the body where it can gain your attention by taking on new life, in order to *make* you deal with it. It is the old, one way or another, dilemma. It seems that stepping up to the plate to deal with the fear is the best way to walk through it. We do not comfort it, but engage it and ask it what it wants of us. How can we calm its Spirit to lead it to a peaceful place? We honor that within the fear is a truth, a real concern, seeking an Allie. If we are to make relationship with that fear, we must seek to make a choice with it for the highest good for all concerned. We are each in the center of that concern. Fear is the reminder to stop on the corner until the light turns green to allow us to cross into a new place of safe knowing.

Even as I wrote this, I was in a huge moment of fear around a family situation. So I decided to make a list of all of the things that I fear, just as soon as I finish the one about all of the things that I love about life. So far, there is no room on the paper for fear. To live my life in fear is not to live at all. To surrender the fear is to give power to the divine gift of choice. This reminder grabs my soul on a regular basis. One of the only tools that I have found to consistently work for me is the *BUT/AND* theory Grandma Barbara once offered to me, that when I am making choices, instead of speaking my choice and saying BUT, (as though there was a reason for the activity NOT to happen...) I was reminded that saying AND as a reason that I WOULD continue to see my choice as a working option. AND it works!!! It allows for the choice to be made. For instance:

I want to write this book, yet, every time I sit down someone calls and I have a new distraction to getting it done. I am the one who chooses to allow the distraction or not.

In this time when the airwaves are filled with violent and sad images of those in crisis, we need to transform fear. When we are seeing police officers in the grocery stores and schools, and children do not feel safe in the local park; we need to transform fear. We look for a magic wand and wait for Mickey Mouse to show up in a wizards cap to make enough brooms to sweep away the mountains of fear all around us. Yet, isn't it each one of us who will sing the song and move the broom to allow the fear to take on a new image in our minds eye? When we call upon the winds to put hope into the breath of fear, we must exhale to make room for that hope to fill our lungs. When we are seeking spiritual food, we need only look as far as the spiritual garden tended by loving hands of a grandmother or young one. It is however each of our choice if we seek to walk within that garden and pick the fruit of healing to fill the vessel that has been emptied of the fears and open to the possibility of a new tomorrow.

It seems that every direction I look to seek the answers, the arrow on the map points to me. It points to my making sound choice. It points to me discerning what situation is going to make me uncomfortable so much that I am paralyzed with fear OR, I can choose the direction on the map that carries me down the road of joyful soul-ution. In any case, the task of transformation lives within me. There is not a transformation spa in the yellow pages that is going to do all of the work for me. I can look to others to ease the pain of the wounds. I can look at them and ask for a new way of seeing or feeling things, AND still it is feeling and me that must do the seeing. An old revolutionary, now Medicine woman, once told me she discovered; *"You cannot fight for peace."* I can reach out and choose which path allows me the comfort of the journey to peace. No one else can walk that walk for me. I am in control of the outcome, as it is MY steps that get me there. In any case, I have found that it seems to be my perception of the situation, which needs as much adjustment as the adjustment of the actual situation, itself! The honest answer to the transformation process is actually all about me being ABLE and WILLING to change how I am viewing the situation and allowing myself to see a non-fear based option to create comfort that my Body, Mind, and Spirit seek to live and walk in balance.

May each of us seek the peace from inside and allow it to emerge into the world. We seek inner calm on chaos filled days. May we each know that we are not alone in our feeling fear. We are certainly not alone in the choices of seeking a productive solution. The healing team is readily available for each of us to access, remembering to *CHOOSE to access* is the challenge of our journey. May we all know the peace of knowing, and in the knowing we are whole.

Fear always comes from what MIGHT HAPPEN. When we let go, something always happens. Yet the rational mind insists on playing; let's make a deal.

LET GO AND ALLOW LIFE TO HAPPEN ON IT'S OWN!

The old folks who walked this planet before us had many reasons they felt the need to discuss fear. They could see fear as the source of loosing all rights and health. They saw fear as a means to control them and keep them for their Spiritual expressions. They had created hundreds of ways to create a safe container for home, health and belief systems some of the 'myths' of the past had become huge obstacles to functioning in today's society. Other practices had been some of the only reasons that they had survived everything from small pox to being relocated in the midst of harsh western winters. In order for them to transform those harsh situations into a lifestyle that was more acceptable, they had to learn to manipulate the energy around them with every positive aspect that they could muster.

The next series of questions blended within the initiations pushed another level of personal and planetary healing. I might note here that my Fire Walk partner for this initiation was a very powerful government official! God laughs.

WHAT ARE YOU PROTECTING?

WHO ARE THE ENEMIES?

*A SEEKER OF TRUTH FOLLOWS NO PATH.
ALL PATHS LEAD TO WHERE THE TRUTH LIVES.*

739,000 people die each year in the US due to medical error and medication mixes in error. According to Noetic Science statistics the main causes of chemical imbalance are pesticides in food, preservatives in food, Msg, aspertaine, sulfa Immunizations, Ritalin, Prozac family of medications, Food allergy, Life trauma and FEAR!

Look at what this list is all about; it is fear. We fear failure, so we push ourselves. Many of us have spent our lives on over-drive and never feeling like we did enough. We fear that we cannot grow more food than all our relations need to share in order to maintain environmental balance, so we poison our own food chain while attempting to protect it. We are afraid we don't have enough time to go to the market a couple of times a week, so we want shelf life to our food for convenience, and more poison. THEN, we worry about getting chronic illness from what we have consumed out of convenience. It takes half our resources to recover from what we did to ourselves, even when we knew better. We have technology all around us to determine what is making us ill. We can do it through blood, saliva, urine tests and even hair tests. We have natural doctors all around us who tell us to eat natural. We spend half of our lives trying to decide what to put into our bodies, and the other half working to maintain it, either through our jobs or our healing practice, or both. When we sleep, we miss most of the powerful dreams, while we dish through our trauma and fears. We build houses of stress and then wonder why we are never feeling WHOLE! On top of it, we are all feeling a deep sense of urgency to live out our Karmic contracts. We see the world falling apart and we want to jump in with some support and some solutions Many of us are just too darn tired and frustrated to see the work through to our highest expectations. We need a team, just like the Grandmas formed.

And there is lies the biggest secret of all. It is the magic of the spider that weaves solutions and makes a call in the winds that we might find the right kindred spirit team. JUST IN TIME!

* BE COMFORTABLE WITH ALL ASPECTS OF LIFE & DEATH
* CELEBRATE ALL ASPECTS OF LIFE
* BE WILLING TO CREATE IN FERTILE FIELDS OF GROWTH
* WE MUST BECOME LIGHTER TO BECOME LIGHT
* FIND A NEW RYTHM TO YOUR SUCCESS

* STRENGTH IS HAVING A RELATIONSHIP WITH YOURSELF
* DISCOVER THE WARRIOR/WARRIORESS INSIDE

The Grams explained that no matter what we do in life, when we place fear into the process we freeze the process and nothing happens. Healing Fear is 80% of what takes place in the gateway of the West, place source of healing waters. With every document they wrote, there was a place of first looking at it from the eyes of the Eagle in the East. They then took the vision to the south and examine what appears to be a Trickster that holds back process. It is how we how to manage those Tricksters to see the task through. Beyond the mantra KISS YOUR MONSTERS ON THE NOSE, was good old fashioned observation and action fueled by passion that allows success through the southern gateway of Coyotes and clowns of life. When we move around the Medicine Wheel to the West we are always standing in a place of purifying away the trauma of the past and the others side of transformation. This is the place of dreaming and inhaling the solutions that come in the night visions.

* WHAT MAKES YOU ILL?
* WHY?
* WHAT HAPPENS WHEN YOU GET ILL?
* WHAT AILMENTS HAVE YOU EXPERIENCED THROUGHOUT LIFE?
* WHAT INJURIES HAVE YOU EXPERIENCED DURING LIFE?
* WHAT IS YOUR VISUAL IMPRINTS OF SIKCNESS AND HEALING?
* AMA DIAGNOSES THROUGHOUT LIFE?
* WHAT ARE THE ORGANS OF COMPLAINT?
* IS THERE A PATTERN FOR HEALING?
* WHAT ARE THE QUESTIONS ASKED OF ORGANS?
* WHAT IS THE PAIN OF STORY/ WHAT DID YOU LEARN FROM THE DISEASE?
* WHAT ELEMENTS WILL YOU TRANSFORM AND HOW?
* WHAT MUST YOU COMPOST?
* WHAT DO YOU WISH TO HARVEST?
* WHAT WILL YOUR FRUIT LOOK LIKE?
* WHAT IS THE, FLOWER OF YOUR VISION?

* WHAT IS THE BUD?

* HOW WILL IT GROW?

* HOW DOES IT SPROUT?

IF YOUR KNOW WHAT YOU WANT IN THIS LIFETIME... THEN DO IT NOW!

JOURNEY TO THE WEST GATE WAY THAT HELPS US HEAL THE FEAR.

This is the place that we look to the healing waters and the waters of rebirth to help us do our work. We cannot do the bigger things, until we attend to what is going on in our internal universe. We must mange our own system, before we can presume to know how to show anyone else how to manage the bigger picture of community and planet. Water is the magical means of movement in stone peoples lodge and the purification and the honoring.. There are waters of the Altars are collected and merged from everyplace the Grams travel. They always share with other water altars with other prayerful keepers of regeneration. Water is the moon ceremony and water-birthing vessel. Water is the keeper the emotions, a woman should feel. The water is the birth and death. It is about balance in your body too much that is diarrhea and not enough is constipation. Working with water can be as simple as remembering that a sea salt bath will glue you back together after an intense confrontation with too much life. Water is about maintaining a flow in our lives, and being able to stop pushing the river.

CONNECTING WITH THE PASSION OF THE WATERS

Luz Clara taught us to set up an Altar and "make love to the Goddess". That is how the visit to the waters should be with THAT someone special in your life. The grandmothers say that we should step into the waters and gently washing each other, chakra by chakra. This creates a place of anticipation and clearing away of old that brings a holy union. That washing should happen in a quiet and special place of fresh waters. The plants and oils and fabrics of the most delicate offerings of the earth, one again unite the elements and transform the inner fires to bring up a whole sharing. This ritual includes the process of making a special new healing tea.

It is that same passion that is stirred behind a Sacred intent, that allows one the alchemy to be a mover and a shaker of vision becoming reality. It is deep within that passion that wholeness lives. She suggests that we make love as an act of ceremony that we offer up to the highest Holy.

PLUNGING INTO THE SACRED WATERS OF PURIFICATION

In many cultures the contrast of being in a sauna and running into the snow or jumping into an ice bath brings on a shock to the system to jump-start many a healing process. For our circle the process involves being in the Sacred Stone People's lodge and then laying in the pure creek waters seven times. Our Cherokee friends like to do this at dawn in the coldest water -falls.

And many of us have been baptized as babies or as young children at some point where a dogma has decided we need to be cleaned off and made accountable for our own sins. We still find ritual use of water as a means to clear and to connect to the source of all life.

GATHERING THE WATERS AND TRANSFORMING THROUGH PRAYER

This process has been shared by women around the world, for me, some of the finest keepers of this Water Altar is Grandma Bertha Burch Grove, Kathy Ravenwood. In their own work they have maintained on this ritual in its finest forms. At each location of fresh water that we visit we go to a to make a prayer for the healthy waters to flow again. . We stir in our intent of offering a clearing for the toxins and placing our healing desires and transforming energy into the waters. We carry a small bottle of water from our own healing altar to offer along with a small gift, and we gather some water to return to our altar at home base.

Golden Eagle Bear taught me to put crystals in this vessel of water and to make new medicine that I used to wash wounds and to wipe shame of fear in the many healing rituals.

Grandma Bertha taught us to take the bottles of drinking water to the lodge and to make Medicine to return to our loved ones back at home. She always recommends fresh spring waters for this process.

Grandpa Wallace had us gather fresh waters at the springs and pray as we bottled it and carried it home to be used in all Sacred cooking and ceremonial rituals of healing with the waters.

Honoring the waters of our source is very important in all aspects of healing. As we move into co-creation of vision; any vision, there is a need for water and all of the emotions to flow, like the peaceful waters of a mountain stream.

The Grams sent me back to Wyoming to the place of my own birth waters to heal the wounds. It was hard, and one of the places I had become very ill. I was told that this bacterial strain came from the waters of the Snake river. Here was another trickster of the south, where I was seeking to rekindle my inner fires.

☾⋆

I CAME HERE SEARCHING
    FOR MY SOUL'S REMNANTS
I FOUND JOY & SORROW
    IN A TEACUP AND A BROOM
I FOUND LINEAGE IN A BOX
    WHERE HOPES ALL ONCE BLOOMED
I FOUND SISTERHOOD
    AND MOTHERHOOD
IN THE ARMS OF THE PAST
    AND PRESENT
I FOUND COMFORT IN FATHER
    BROTHER AND THE ROOTS OF SAGE
I FOUND BOXES AND SMELLS
    DEAD FLOWERS AND HOPES THAT FAILED
I FOUND LIFE AND DEATH IN
    A COWBOY JUBILEE
I FOUND LOTS OF LITTLE PARTS OF ME.

JOURNEY SIX

Strength comes from Commitment

The Grams always told me that the words commitment was the biggest in the dictionary. When making a commitment to Spirit, we are making a date with our own purpose and growth. We always keep our commitments no matter how hard they are to see through to the end result. We make commitments to prepare for all major rituals and rites of passage. Each commitment involves the preparation and support of the process, be it a ceremony or an intending of a goal like building a Healing center or outreach program. There is no point in making a commitment to anything that you're not willing to work towards each and every day.

LOOK NOT FROM THE MIND,
                       BUT FROM THE SOUL!!!

Feel
        Experience
                Choices
                        Evolve

HOW DO YOU LOOK AT YOUR COMMITMENT?

HOW DOES SPIRIT LOOK AT YOUR COMMITMENT?

HOW IN TOUCH ARE YOU WITH GIVING AND RECEIVING?

THE ART OF SPIRITUAL COMPOST

It's all around us as the trees drop their leaves and the garden is turned to the winter phase. Little forms of Shamanic death are everywhere we look. The flowers have pretty much stopped blooming, and we can barely see the road for the wind blown limbs of trees and all forms of natures droppings. Some of the wisest animals have burrowed in for the season and won't be back until February; along with the new leaves, flowers and blooms of spring. Somehow we know that is a truth. No matter what the Earth Changes news is, we seem to have a knowing in our heart that Spring WILL return and we will be planting and harvesting all over again. YET, even in that knowing, there is a longing for reassurance that the things around us that we take for granted, will remain loyal and do what we know is supposed to happen in each cycle of the moon. We look at the dogwoods and roses, and remind them as we trim them back, that we are expecting them to grow again next year, no matter what global warming does. We call to the Bees and ask them to remember to buzz around the garden again, and the critters to raid the trash again. Because, in our hearts and minds we KNOW that is what is supposed to happen. Nature takes its course over and over again.

My favorite garden GURU, Mark Hallert has the most amazing garden out in Oregon. I thrill each year to run into that garden and harvest the berries and stand next to the flowers that are taller than me. I literally get lost in his garden. I have now seen that garden in all of its phases, and there are not always berries and flowers taller than me. There is a dormant time while he works the soil. You know the stuff deep in the mama's gut that will feed and nurture the garden next season. I call it Mark's religion of compost. It is where we start in the kitchen preparing the foods and praying over them. We nurture from the foods and left over's as long as we can. Then the last of the leftovers go into the compost bucket. We make a little prayer as we add it to the processing pile out doors and then in the spring we gather that special soil that we have created and mix it into our garden as we get ready to plant, all over again. We pray on the garden each day and pray really wonderful thanks as we harvest to take it to the kitchen to........you get it. It is a cycle of life and prayers and nurturing.

So, just where am I going with this Geez Charla, we all know this ? It is about our own Spiritual composting time. In the past week I have spoken to over a dozen close friends and Elders who are feeling more than a little funky. They are tired, Spiritually butt kicked and emotionally dry of the juices that fed the people all ceremonial season. AND, as brilliant and enlightened as we all are, we forget that in our life cycle, in our Shamanic practice cycle; WE ARE SUPPOSED TO BE DOWN FOR THIS CYCLE OF HEALING, PRAYING, VISIONING, AND COMPOSTING ALL OF THE GOOD AND THE LEFT OVER EMOTIONS FROM THE PAST SEASON! This is the time of the year that we are supposed to sit back and evaluate what has worked, not worked and what we chose to carry forward into the next season. This is the time when we do sit back with our Spiritual PTSD and heal the wounds of so many around us. We must clean the sticky stuff that we all carried home in the process of our work. And darn it, that just hurts sometimes. It is near impossible to honestly touch into the heart and soul of the people and not feel what we are all feeling right now.

So, like the rest of you. I have been very quiet. I unplugged the phone for many days. I took long naps and dusted the shelves in the house and in my mind. I shuffled through the house and the land slowly and shed a few tears over the losses of so many that we had not had time to focus on any form of grief. I will work my way around to the celebration point. First I must stop to go within, grieve, feel and hold a composting funeral for all of the leftover emotions. If I don't, just like food left too long in the refrigerator ; it will rot inside of me, not be offered into next years garden. AND friends, even as I know it is a truth of the process of my Spiritual growing to go back inside myself and turn over the garden. The turning is a bit upsetting. That garden was so abundant in the height of the ceremonial season and now it is fallow. The depth of the energy that fed it each day is gone. The laughter of the children cannot be heard on the land. The busy chatter of the staff is missing. The waves of energy from the lodges and the arrival of special guests are not there. The rush is gone, and it feels like a long flat line of who cares. Yep, that is me, every single November and December as I sit back to put together the plans for the coming year.

Back into the day, when the corporations owned my soul, we did the same thing. This was the time of the year when we crunched the numbers and set the goals. ONLY instead of sitting back to vision... We fussed and flustered as we fought to shift the cycles of the season and make the winter months more productive to the bottom line. We fought the cold and flu season and made ourselves ill by working too hard when we were supposed to be resting. We did not compost the harvest, but spread it as far as we could and then chewed out the staff for everything getting naturally, slow.

This is a time for us to feel. There is a lot to feel. There is a place for each of us to look in the mirror and see new lines in our faces and more gray hair. It is a time to pull out of the spin and look at what we created while we were spinning so fast. The slowing down to many looks and feels like depression. It is. The word in the dictionary says that depression is when our energy is stagnant. Which simply means the energy that we bring up to work on others is not flowing as fast as it was when we were jumping through flaming hoops for the ceremonies all season. In other words…WE ARE SUPPOSED TO BE STAGNANT RIGHT NOW AS A NATURAL PROCESS OF COMPOSTING SO WE CAN PLANT NEW GARDENS NEXT YEAR. Hey the skunks are smart enough to figure this out, and no one gave them a pill because they crawled into the earth and shut everyone out until things warm up again. Why are we not as smart as the skunks?

This past year I/we at Hawkwind served more folks than ever before. I saw the same in most of my Elder friends. The circles were big and they were intense. The world situation is intense, and if we are the wisdom keepers, the spinners, the magicians and transformers of change; WE ARE SUPPOSED TO FEEL THIS, so we can work it. And yes there is a place to rest from feeling, so it is not too overwhelming. Like many of you, I stopped sleeping through the night quite some time ago. When my medicine father was making his passage he taught me the power of the time between 3am and 6am, and I began to use it. Then I lost my ability to get a full night of sleep. I, like hundreds around me was not getting sufficient dreamtime. Many of my old herbal allies were not working, and I tried a couple of meds. Waking up with a headache and cotton in my brain was not allowing the flow of clear energy. And HEY, I am an energy junkie, so I want my pure energy juice to be flowing. I love the juicy dreams that guide my wisest choices, and I am not real thrilled when I am feeling shaky and achy from lack of rest. So, like my compost pile where I add some hay to the process of breaking it all down; I have been adding herbal teas to my day. In particular I have been doing infusions of oat straw and nettles with some red clover or raspberry. I put a CD of gentle music on, and I stay there until I know I have had 7 hours of sleep. If I get up, I may have some Chamomile tea, but I go right back into the darkness and maybe even play the CD again. It makes a huge difference. And yes, I know that I am composting my internal garden right now. I am processing, and it is okay to do that. Actually it is part of my evolutionary job.

If you are one out there feeling the funk, I honor you. I thank you. You are doing your job right now. I know I will see you again when the skunks come back out. I know you will be perky and pretty and full of juice. If you are feeling funkier than usual, I encourage you not to watch the news. Stay out of the clustered airports and malls. Avoid department stores and crowds filled with stress and backed by muzak. Stay in your natural place. Nest, sleep, read, journal, take a vision quest inside your own soul and seek the means to step back out next year. The prophecies and the economists predict next year could begin a cycle of a really rough ride. If you had trouble paying for gas to travel this year, add to the budget for next year. There isn't going to be more gas or more natural resources again in our lifetime. So if it is pinching your reality now, step back, step within and see what is really important to plant in that garden next year. No reason to plan on putting your energy into things that did not and do not continue to work. AND MOST OF ALL, you won't have any energy to plant and work that garden if you do not rest, remorse, refuel, restore and renew. It is simply what you are supposed to be doing right now. Don't be embarrassed. There is no shame to be feeling what your experience right now. It is real and it means you feel. Thank God we all still feel.

Today, I honor each of you. Today I rest and feel. I prepare to vision in the longest night. I mean really folks, how many more Solstices will offer you that portal in you lifetime? There are only five more between now and 2012 that we are supposed to use to transform the planet into a new reality. FINE, there is no stress. So lets not waste our depression time, lets use it as the means to warm up the compost for the new garden that we will plant for the generations to come. Lets lay back and wallow in it for a minute…just a long minute. And then we shake it and move into the next cycle. Right now, we don't even have to know what that cycle looks like. Not any more than the dogwood tree outside my door. It is bare right now. It is stiff and cold. I see it in its beauty and full of blooms, when its time is right. Lets respect for our shared composting time. That is a big wisdom that comes from living enough time to honor the north gateway of wisdom. The north gateway also teaches us what to do with those herbs and plants once they have bloomed. It includes the power of the minerals, bones, woods and the tree that created this earth. It is in the stones, medicine wheels, jewelry North is the buffalo and strength. The north gateway is courage, wisdom and endurance. Earth is our prosperity and abundance and all that nurtures us. Earth is our logic base.

At this time in my own life, I am seeking every form of logic, both of the mundane and of the magical realm to allow me to see my path clear to wholeness.

> "I DO CHOOSE TO LIVE A NON-ORDINARY LIFE IN AN ORDINARY WORLD…geez, I live in Alabama for God's sake."

I begin to examine my own commitments. I had been loyal to a fault all of my life. I was the kind of girl that made a commitment and kept it, no matter how bad it hurt. All of my life I had made strong commitments to everyone around me, accept myself. Certainly that may be a universal truth for many of us, and today it was important for me to recognize the need to commit as much love and devotion to my own vision as I had given to everyone else's. I knew that the choices I made in this moment would effect how I viewed my final report card when I left this world.

I prepare to head for SHIP (This is a Shamanic breath work program that takes nine months of intensive work to complete.) with this knowing of my shamanic shattering, and a Blue Star bundle that talks to me each night about the ways to resolve my inner issues. I have my white flag of surrender in hand and drive my weak and shaky body to North Carolina begging for help.

When I get there I feel more awkward that I have in years. I have not walked into the great unknown like this any other time than SUN DANCE. This feels every bit as intimidating as that Lakota process. However, here I know I will be fed and held, not purged and left to process alone. Within the first hour I am feeling like the odd girl out and perhaps I had made a wrong choice. After the opening circle I hike up the hill to the cabin I was staying in, and prayed with The Blue Star Bundle again. I heard in my heart the need to stay. So I did, however reluctant to the process that made me feel so naked in front of others.

I keep hearing the word INTEGRITY. So I deal with all of the raw emotions and press ahead. My first breath work comes on the anniversary of my medicine father's death four years before. It is that final day of the CURSE he put on all of his ceremonial tools, because he knew they would be stolen. It was why I did not want them, and had allowed the best parts of the tools he offered me as his POA to live in my heart. All of this story of his tools, the family history and the ups and downs of his fame had been part of my secret of being his adopted daughter. As I did that first breath work the most horrible aspects of my life came up in my face. My childhood was raw in that moment. My years of searching for the right healing answers felt a complete failure as I admitted the depth of my fear and frustration that choked my breath away. The pain was over the top and I felt as though my head was going to explode from the agony. Now I really wanted to leave, but the snows came in and I could barely get up and down the hill, much less try to figure out how to drive through the canyon. I head back to my cabin and clutch the bundle and cry through the night, alone.

BECOME THE CHANGE YOU WISH TO BE, GRANDDAUGHTER. YOU HAVE HIT A PEAK OF EVOLUTION, HEAL THE WOUND AND LET GO OF THE PAST.

I step out into the Star filled sky and reach out to tell the old Medicine- man of my past goodbye, one more time and pace through the night trying to figure out how to let go out what binds me to the old paradigm of pain, shame and suffering. I know better, yet I somehow am not seeing my way clear of the obvious.

STRENGTH, COURAGE, CREATIVITY, move beyond OPPRESSION...

It sounded good, but I was not feeling it in my ailing cells. I worked every series of questions these old ones had asked. I asked them at the water. I cried them at the fire. I walked them and danced them into the earth. I sang them and gasped for more air. I reached for spirit with honest intent. Then I sat back and waited and listened.

WHAT AND WHO ARE THE PROTECTORS????

I REALIZE THAT MY FIRST SHAMANIC DEATH TOOK PLACE THE DAY I WAS BORN. I have a life -time of issues I have not resolved. I need to let go and begin, again. The bundle tells me it is time to lead my own REAL life, and this is my seventh SHAMANIC DEATH and the one that would carry me to my Wisdom. I am hoping that wisdom will come in aged and gentle ways and I will recognize it as it reaches out to hold me.

When I show tolerance to intolerance, that is what I get back....

You have to have a self to be selfish....dahhhh

These little pieces of wisdom dropped in through out the night and into the next day. More snow kept me there, even though I wanted to run. I entered the room ready to tell everyone I could not finish the program, when one of the three men began to share his story. It was the one man I thought to be the odd man out in the room. He was from my southern county and reeked of Southern religion and conflicted man. All of a sudden as he told his story, and he was me. As he told about a child running from abuse, I was the child running in fear. Even when my feet aren't moving, I knew it was my fear that have my legs shaking trying to run. Then the next woman spoke, and she was my fear as a mother. The next one speaks and she is my guilt and shame. This went on all around the circle until it came to me. I knew I was everyone in that room and more and must stay as if to put the puzzle of me back together again. I suddenly knew that for the first time in years I honestly had support to put that puzzle together, and I began to settle into my body and really breathe. My mind spins and the air is filled with more questions than answers.

WHAT IS A SIN? Judith begins my new questions.

Being powerful is not an act of being selfish. I keep working the work in my heart and soul to acknowledge the power that is rightfully mine.

Time to step on the FORGIVENESS BUS again.

I get help dealing with the issues of being deemed unworthy by the Mormons and all of my family. It is a break through day for me. I am able to begin to focus on the TRUTH of my story and to outline the many aspects of my childhood that I had buried under my pillow for far too long. A biofeedback and acupuncture session relieves the pain enough that I can move into the real process of re-birthing. I realize that I have been trapped in the womb hiding in pain and must really work to get beyond that place where I am afraid to just be alive and breathe. Getting to know air as an ally was pushing way more buttons than I anticipated.

WHAT IS FREEDOM?

My journal begins to fill with letters of forgiveness to my mom and dad. I begin to write it to the bones and feel with every aspect of my being the choices between pain and calm. I begin to list everything that nurtures my soul.

ACCOUNTABILITY IS MORE IMPORTANT THAN RESPONSIBILITY. My Spiritual checkbook is way out of balance.

I manage to find enough humor in it all to come up with a fun ritual that honors my own emergence out of the shadows into the light. Yet, I know that I have been safe to make fun of it in this circle, and I must go home to do the serious work and be very honest with my mates at Hawkwind. Sure I have discovered that it all had to do with a wonky birth and bad baby formula. Sure we should all string Dr. Spock up and beat him for the manner in which children of the 50's were raised. But that is over. What I must do now is damage control and letting go of all of childhood trauma.

I begin the colon cleanse and detox at a deeper level and spend the next few weeks in the bathroom. At the same time I begin to clean my home and ceremonial connections with a new focus. Peel away that which is not needed. This include Medicine bundles given to me by men and warriors that are not appropriate to my journey/ these men had been warriors attached to the war, that I was choosing to transform. I began to feel the lightness take over the burdens of the past.

HOPE FOR THE BEST, MAKE PEACE WITH THE REST...

The Grams inspiration is lacking in my heart. I attempted peace, yet all I could feel was the chaos. I reached out beyond the instructions of the old ones and found some new and very important tools to add to my Medicine bundle.

FIVE CYCLES OF CHANGE, By Linda Star Wolf

30 QUESTIONS FOR HUMANITY, By Linda Star wolf

EMPOWERING THE SPIRIT, By Judith Corvin-Blackburn

THE HEALERS MANUAL, By Ted Andrews

ALCHEMCIAL HEALING, and POWER ANIMAL MEDIATIONS, By Nicki Scully

WHITE BULLAFO WOMAN IS CALLING, By Brooke Medicine Eagle

I begin the process of the 30 questions with my partner, Judith. We are a perfect match and are equally dedicated to the process. She is a good pal to be able to talk to twice a week, and I am deep into the healing of every cell of my being. This is a high stakes game of survival and I am determined to survive. It is good to have a partner to talk it through. It certainly gets one past the excuses for not activating the work that we all know is imperative to feel wholeness.

WHAT AM I STILL PRETENDING? .....oh dear now I am in trouble.

WHAT DOES MY COLON WANT ME TO KNOW?...oh oh I'm in deep shit

WHAT IS TOXIC IN MY LIFE?....well damn some stuff has to go, sugar and dairy

At this point several of my Elders pass on. They are three whom I have cared for over 15 years. My load gets lighter, and my sorrow deeper. I say good-bye to Aunt Coreen the Dawn Star woman, and feel her merge with my soul. The fact that I can feel my soul is a plus. I hold that Blue Star Bundle and ask her what I am to do. That night my Sun Dance sponsor of many years, Aunt Coreen comes in a dream:

THIS BUNDLE GUIDES YOU DAUGHTER. THIS BUNDLE WILL TAKE YOU HOME TO YOUR SOUL, BUT IT IS NOT YOURS. IT IS JUST PART OF THE JOURNEY. YOU WILL MAKE A NEW BUNDLE OF BLUE PIPE STONE WITH AN OTTER. YOU WILL LEARN TO SWIM IN NEW WATERS AND BECOME THE PLAYFUL CHILD THAT YOU HAVE NEVER BEEN. YOU WILL TEACH OTHERS THE POWER OF REGENERATION WITH YOUR HEART AND YOUR GLEEFUL PRESENCE. YOU HAVE A NEW CHALLENGE, THE ONE THAT TAKES YOU TO JOY. THERE IS ANOTHER WHO WILL CARRY THIS FORWARD, AND ANOTHER AND ANOTHER. RIGHT NOW, YOU WILL COMPLETE. PART OF THE COMPLETION IS TO GATHER THE STORY OF HEALING AND TO FIND THE NEXT WOMAN WHO WILL MOVE FORWARD INTO HE SPIRAL OF LEADING THE PEOPLE THROUGH THE 2012 PORTAL. EACH OF YOU HAS A PART OF THIS PUZZLE. YOU KNOW THAT SHE MUST BE A WISE WOMAN. AS YOU FIND HER, YOU WILL ALSO HAVE TO LET GO OF THOSE WHO WILL NOT CARRY WISDOM FORWARD IN THIS MANNER. YOU WILL MISS THEM, LIKE MANY OF THE BUNDLES THAT YOU WILL LET GO OF. YOU WILL NOT WAIT UNTIL DEATH TO PASS THIS ON. YOU CANNOT LEAVE IT ALL TO ONE PERSON TO CLEAR. IT IS TOO MUCH . YOU MUST CUT THE CORDS THAT BIND AND YOU ARE NOT DONE YET.

The next morning I write to every woman I know who is 55 and over and pose the transfer of the Blue Star bundle. Four women refuse before lunch and one only wants it if it means she will become a real Medicine Woman and be filled with Power. I pause and continue to hold it close in protection of the sacred ways that have been passed on for me to keep alive. I know that if I am to honor my own individual Medicine, that one day I need to pass on every item that has been left in my keeping. I begin to share the treasures with each cycle of the moon.

By now I have shifted from medications to almost all herbs. I am seeing an osteopath, a homeopathic doctor, two acupuncturists, a chiropractor and the AMA type who has just announced that he gives up and wants me to see an infectious disease specialist. He is telling me I need to take five meds at once, and that I have moved into critical state. I follow up with the nutritionist and shift most of my herbs and supplements and take bigger step into a diet with less food that agitates my digestion. I am down to less than 15 foods, and I am spending hours in the bathroom working through my shit. I need to find a way to do this with less expense involved, but know that right now it is all life and death, so I must become my number one priority.

It is time to join Ms. Edwene Gaines for our annual DARK SIDE process and fire walk. I am weak but determined to get through this interaction with other women. The night before the workshop, Mz. Imani and her apprentice Bella show up wanting me to go to Marti Gras. I have never been and would love to go, but know that I am weak and not ready to deal with crowds or New Orleans food. What I am ready to deal with is to let go of one more bundle. The Bundle of the Cobra that is all about sexual wounds wants to go with Mz. Imani. We do a deep ritual and pass it on. Again I lighten the load. I can feel this one leave my gut as she pulls out to head for the NOLO madness. Imani stays behind long enough to help me with a clearing and salt bath, and I am lighter as she heads down the road.

After they leave Gram Twlya comes in a dream. She reminds me I am one of her Peace Elders, and that I have three items that came from her. I should use them and a fourth was coming when I pass on the Blue Star Bundle, she knows the Bundle. She knows the work. She reminds me she had led me to my own tribe, and now I had found many of its members. Work with that support system. She begins to grill me...

HAD I GIVEN MYSELF UNHOLY EXPECTATIONS OF BEING A HOLY WOMAN?

What do you reclaim...renew....rebirth...rejoice...rebel....????
I wake up and write a piece about how I am feeling:

I'm a mom and a grand-mom

I'm a gatekeeper and bundle carrier of prophecy

I'm a writer & producer of many skills

I'm a teacher and facilitator

I'm a wife and sometimes lover by choice

I'm a gardener of delight

I'm a healer and a friend

I'm a Sis-star and I am able to take direction from Spirit.

I hear you Grandma, I hear you.

Peace, Peace, Peace, I hear the wise woman calling, I can hear Jeri sing....

Time to awaken the Heart!!!!

I dream that night and the Old Crone comes and reminds me that as a Mormon I had been raised with the GIVING on one Hand and on the other, the constant fear of not having enough. I had maintained HAWKWIND WITH A SCARCITY EGO, without even knowing it. I have taught THE EARTH CHANGES ARE COMING, and how to suffer through the Sun Dance for so long, that I had become the scarcity, the earth changes and the FEAR.

NO way, is that what I could honestly see in the mirror. Is that why I lead workshop after workshop and had either a no show audience or received little or no pay. WHERE IS THE BALANCE BETWEEN OFFERING CEREMONY AT NO COST, AND THE HEALING RITUAL THAT I TEACH AND OFFER ON A DAILY BASIS?

What is limit ?
What is expansion?

Isn't balance that places you find in the center of space and time?

I begin to list what lives within my collective belief system......
Like; JESUS WASN'T SUPPOSED TO HAVE FUN
EVERYTHING HAPPENS FOR A REASON
NICE GIRLS DON'T.....(fill in the blank)
YOU CAN DO ANYTHING YOU WANT, BUT YOU HAD BETTER MAKE THE RIGHT CHOICE!

BE AUTHENTIC BUT DON'T MAKE WAVES

BE STRONG…DON'T SHOW EMOTION

YOU'RE TOO DISTANT…TOO FOCUSED…TOO ORGANIZED…Please help me organize this project.

DO WHAT YOU DO ON PURPOSE AND UNDERSTAND THE PURPOSE…..I am getting more confused with each suggestion.

EACH DAY, I AM TRANSFORMING CELLS.

I EXPAND AND TAKE NEW PERSPECTIVE.

I DELIGHT IN GOD'S TIMING.

I AM THE PEACE I HAVE BEEN LOOKING FOR !

I EXAMINE I THE REALITY I HAVE COME TO KNOW WITH NEW EYES.

I MUSE AT THE MEMORIES IN THE SOLES OF MY FEET, KNOWING THEY HAVE WALKED THROUGH MANY GATEWAYS. WHAT MEMORY IS IMPORTANT TO WALK FORWARD WITH INTO OUR NEW TOMORROWS?

BE HERE ...NOW!

I WANDER FROM ROCK TO ROCK

STONE TO STONE

UP THE MOUNTAIN TRAIL

STEEP AND ROCKY

I GO POINT TO POINT

MARKER TO MARKER

UP THE STEEP TRAIL OF LIFE

WONDERING ABOUT

THE POINTS I COME TO

MAKE ME STOP AND BREATHE

I DON'T ALWAYS STOP

TO HEAR THE ANSWERS AROUND ME

I ASK , Why?

JOURNAL THOUGHTS ON YOUR OWN PURPOSE:

JOURNEY SEVEN

Endurance of the Magical Journey

It has been my experience that we are all looking for the Magical journey. It may have started the first time we read *Pippy Long Stocking* or a book of great childhood fantasy. It may have come from some TV suggestion. Where -ever the desires formed, it is the journey of how we satisfy those desires that seems to make up life. For myself, creating adventure has been a life long pleasure and endurance. That did begin in the back rooms of a musty Wyoming library. Oh sure, I was surrounded with the wisdom of the natives of the area; I just didn't know it. Thus I always looked beyond my own back yard. By the time I reached that magical year of fifty-six, I had a room filled with journals, files of ancient memories and archives of old ones who had wanted to keep some wisdom alive. This Blue Star bundle was one of over a dozen in my hands at the time. Each one had come with some specific instructions. Yet, the Blue Star Bundle seemed to be more than that. It wasn't all about me keeping someone else's vision alive, it was about me finding and embracing my own vision.

Yes, it came with some amazing insights and instructions. There were four Atlars to the East that were dedicated to the clarity that comes from the eyes of the Eagle and the ability to fly over life's challenges. They could be used for the Stone People's Lodge or prayer rituals. There were four Altars to the south fires and the spider as a weaver of new dreams. Yet, there were altars that revealed the shadows of life and the hidden places of the soul. These Altars are only used for rare situations like Ghost Sickness or lost things, like our minds or spirit. There were four Altars to the West using the Sacred Waters and the night Medicine for healing and transforming the disease that is all around us. There were four Altars to the Thunders and the power of the energy we use to awaken the heart to new creation. There were four more Altars to the North that were dedicated to wisdom and being keepers of the sacred family. They worked with courage and putting an end to the wars inside and out. There were four more Altars to work with the plants and animals of earth. Another four Altars were dedicated to the sun, moon and stars of the sky. I stood in the center as the Altar that binds all of the magical formula. I could sweat, pray, dance and quest and maybe something would happen. Yet, I knew nothing real would happen until

I could find and activate my own heart in the center of it all. Otherwise, I was simply sitti. in another library reading about how someone else did it. These old Grandmothers of my past insisted that I get up and do it. They demanded that I get up and live, or stop wasting God's time.

Thus, I followed the list of instructions. I went from ritual to ritual, always seeking and making notes of what I thought I had just discovered for the first time. Then I would go back and look in the notes and see how many ways they had tried to teach me that in my spunky youth. Maybe it takes fifty-six years to clear the ear-wax enough to hear the voice of Spirit.

The clues they gave me were many. They set times for ritual that were when the portals were open and the veil of time is thin. They suggested that I learn the many aspects that each star system teaches us. They indicated that I should set up my Altars at power times; Dusk, Dawn and 3:23 am. I should amplify this with working on the full moon, new moon, equinox and solstice at the crossing points in time.

Support tools FOR THE BLUE STAR ALTARS:

6x HERKIMER DIAMOND	6x MOLDIVITE
6x ROSE QUARTZ	1x METORITE
6x BLUE SAPPHIRE	1x DIAMOND
6x AMETHYST	6x TURQUOISE
6X HEMATITIE	6x TURQUOISE
6X EMERALD	1X SILVER
1x NIOBIAN METAL	1x GOLD
1X TITANIUM METAL	1X COPPER
1X BLOODSTONE or RED CYRSTAL	
1X CLEAR QUARTZ CRYSTAL GENERATOR	

Prepare for your final initiation:

Altar Cloth

Altar Case

Special Rattle

Special Drum

nunpa

ade of Blue Macaw feathers

: osha, cedar, sage, sweetgrass, lavendar, amber and dragons blood.

9x candles; red, yellow, black, white, purple. blue, green silver, gold

Ceremonial Regalia to honor the Blue Star

Symbols of the animals and allies that carry you forward

Everything should be prepared with the cycles of the moon and with natural materials. Each object should carry a story that connects to the vision of wholeness. Every items should be cleared and hnonored for the life it is offering to you. Look at all of the connections as you weave the bundle together. Note what order items come to you and if you are receiving more items of water than fire or more of a particular animal. Look for your own signs and signets of your energy field. What you call in is what you will need to create this magical bundle that speaks of you and your power as a keeper of Medicine.

CEREMONIAL OBJECTS TO PREPARE:

Of Earth: This is the Altar that includes the working of the Stone People's Lodge and Cannunpa Wakan. It is the place to come to work within the Medicine Wheel, and with the plants and animals. It is where we make relationship with the womb of the mother that holds us here. This is where we learn the proper plants for smudge and for intake into the body that is filled with toxins. This is where we learn to use the stones as generators of energetic influence. This is the place we learn to manage the bones of our bodies and how we nurture them and use them in our earth walk. This is the place on the Altar for our family and our spiritual food. The tools we prepare are basic. We prepare them in the old way of working the energy of the moon and sun and working with the gentle ways of the earth.

We make a special Altar Cloth, Talking stick, Cannunpa, Regalia of the leathers and animals. We gather small stones of our knowing, and the plants of our healing. We prepare our wooden bucket and find the perfect antlers for carrying the volcanic stones to the lodge. We use our clan and family symbols to identify our energy as we make our transformational magic.

Of Water: We create a special water vessel and water stones, water animals and cleansing rituals. We have our special water drums and water prayers. We use the special waters to wash the wounds and to offer healing to the primordial fluids of life. Always gather from the sources of water.

Of Fire: We make our drum and add the passion of our heartbeat, we find the song that came with the dogs and Coyotes,. We hear the tones of passion that keep us alive. We make our prayer ties and prayer robes to hang as a call to spirit. We make masks and robes of shame as a means to transform our way of seeing and being. We make our fire without fuels and work with sulfer to transform the old angers, fears, shames and sorrows into hope and opportunity for the younger ones, yet to come.

Of Air: Smudging fan, rattle of the voice of Spirit (one for each element) We make our feather fans and sing the dawn star songs. We learn to listen and to pray with new voice. We learn our dances and work our trances. We use air as movement and breath of life. We paint the birch bundles and connect to the power of the trees and the winds. We make baskets to hold the gifts of life. We learn to speak the truth and we learn the power of silence.

Of Stars: We prepare the Star Quilt, along with the shawl of the Grandmother. We prepare the symbols of our journey from the first star that brought us here to all of the shining stars in our life. This is the place of RE-MEMBERING. We do that with symbols and signets of time. We use the metals and candles to hold the light. We use color and sound, and we ignite our work with a deep connect to SELF. We weave a tapestry that speaks of our journey and the love that we will leave behind when we go. There are new tools of the Stars like the Hang and the bells.

Of Spirit: We offer bowls of special prepared foods to feed the spirits before we ask them to feed us. We make gifts of the soul to friends, family and to those we wish to forgive. We connect with our source, by taking time to honor each aspect of our life. We honor that life, BEFORE we ask it to do something more amazing than just being here. We honor that being here is enough and doing more is a gift that we earn and we maintain with integrity. It is all about the balance. No one person should get to do so much that there is nothing left for the next Spiritual over achiever to fix.

We must come to know what works for each of us. It does us no good to know how it worked for Merlin, if we cannot ignite that magic in our own lives. We can have every tool made to perfection, yet it is the perfection that lives inside of us that made the tool. We need to be able to do the work with empty hands and open heart. The tools are just tools, and they can get in the way, unless we become the Altar and become the tool of transformation.

CEREMONIAL MESA'S & ALTARS; We create the Medicine bag filled with the memories and life. We add stones and sands of sacred places. We add pieces of the journey that we carry with us as part of our magical container. To the Medicine Bundle we add that which is made of a special leather of fabric of our journey. It contains our tools of Cannunpa, rattle, feathers, stones and bones. We add that to our Medicine Altar, which carries something of every element and ally that makes up a particular recipe for response. One bundle may be for teaching, another for healing certain aspects of life. Another Altar may be dedicated to courage of the warrior, or marriage, baby blessings. Every altar carries something of each element, it is the intending and the nature of what is deemed special to that intent that makes the sacred bundle your own special recipe for transformation.

We all have Altars in our home. The Altar may be surrounded with family photos or feathers, leathers, stones and bones of our ancestors. We all have office Altars that are on our computer or window- sill that holds our awards and treasure maps of goals set to allow us a perceived success in your chosen vocation. You might put special power pieces on this Altar that amplify your desires for abundance that is balanced with your giving.

We all tend to set up Altars in our community as we set up sheltering programs, volunteer programs, and service to those in need. We use these tools and bundles as we enter specific gateways and portals.

Some of us delight in portal surfing. This basically means we find windows of opportunity, where the universe amplifies a magnetic force field. This allows the magical process to take on the co-creation of life, much faster and with a stronger impact for the purpose of feeding the body, mind and spirit with the ways of conjuring with good intent. Many of us look for sacred portals around the world that are lined up in a grid-work pattern. We find these places at pyramids and Temples around the world. Then there are those of us who create sacred portals infused with the magical intendings of our own generation. These can be found in our Medicine Wheels, Stone People's lodges, Labyrinths, and new temples of our time. When we take our tools into these specific gateways, we amplify the activation of the work. Thus you find crazy folks with crystals in their pockets, all over the world. We can find that the masters of all religion and even corporate practice have mastered some form of portal surfing. These portals are where we go to alter space and time. It is where we go to return back to the healthy cells in the body to restore These transformational portals are the place we visit for Shamanic death and rebirth. These portals are within the ethers and become a state of mind, as well as a specific location that has a code on the lock. The code might only open on 11:11 or at Summer Solstice. Knowing where and where to portal surf, becomes the skill of the master transformer.

The Shaman uses the portals to empower the ceremonial tools being created. Making a tool of all natural materials within the cycles of the moon or seasons, gives it a specific energy. Oh sure, you can buy lots of these tools, yet it is in the making of them that allows them to carry your

energy forward. And, when we are gifted tools by other Elders, we also inherit the ch[oices]
choices they made while using that tool. Knowing how to clear old energy is prett[y]
with working with tools created by others. It is important that we understand the as[pects of]
animals parts used and how they were harvested. The same would go for the use of her[bs]
and even roots to dye fabrics. There is a proper timing to everything and a sacred math is part of the Shamanic process.

Our ceremonial regalia signifies our training and lineage. It says as much about our skills and mastership as any other tools we create. Many can embarrass themselves with showing up on a struggling reservation over dressed like some Indian princess. The old Grams who made the biggest changes, dressed simple and respectful and saved the big stuff for high ceremony and tribal councils. The creation of the regalia honors the colors of the clan and the phases of life. For instance the child might wear white, while the maiden is dressed in red and the mother in greens or blues. The Grandmother might be in blacks or purples. There are different colors for different events and rituals. It is always good to check ahead and see what is the standard of dress and the proper protocol for entering into the ritual with an Elder. Layers of beads tell stories. Colors and designs tell of Medicine that is being carried. When I see a Lakota man at a dance dressed in white and black or yellow and black; I prepare myself for a dance with the tricksters and my shadows.

Mandalas of the star patterns were offered as a mean to write in names and attributes of the energy that you wish to inspire. Coloring the Mandalas infuses them with life and intent. It is a meditation and calls up certain energies to surround your transformation.

The 5-pointed Star is to form the aura of the body. Enhancing the colors, fills in the places that you may be lacking wholeness of cells.

6-Pointed Star, to hold the vessel of knowledge as influenced in our own life. There is a point for each major form of Medicine or lineage we carry forward. Look around you and see who has touched your life. I had a place on my star for the Lakota ways we practice in our home. There is a point on the star for my Alchemical work as I practice it with Nicki Scully. There is another for my place in the lineage of Sis-Stars of two ancient Star Councils. There is a point dedicated to my work at Isis Cove and the breath work and Star Wolf. Another point on the star is for work with the Blue Otter Grams. I sit in the center and hold my integrity. My Medicine is only as strong as the experience I have allowed AND the heart felt manner in which I deliver it!

7-Pointed Star, holds the power of the Mystic and the healer. This is the one I work with when I begin to see another and to bring color into their world of wholeness.

8-Pointed Star is to awaken the balance of the four directions above and below. It is to form the Caduceus of transformation. This can be found in many forms of working Medicine. It is the fire that connects to the lodge. It is the dance as we spiral around the tree or fires of life. It is the balance of male and female. This star pattern offers a framework for a strong balance between vision and reality.

9-Pointed Star, this will connect us to the Council of all nations, the Eniad of our own souls' purpose. We constantly look into this Council to seek the inner advice. It might happen in our oracle cards, or as we trance and go to the fires of the old ones to seek wisdom. We place nine allies in this star for our above connections to the ancient ones like Isis, Mary or Christ and Buddha. We have a Council of nine who lives below us that have touched our lives in this Earth walk. Those are the ones like Pir Viliat, the Dali Llama, Sun Bear, Grandma Grace and Grandpa Wallace, the Hunas, and masters of our time. We have another council that is around us. Who are the 9 most trusted friends and family that we call when we need to dialog and connect to support of the bigger vision,

11- pointed Star, is a portal of transformation and a crossroads between space and time. Use the 11's to your advantage. We look for the 11:11 frequencies all around us in dates and times to find gateways that carry the frequency to higher realms.

12 Pointed Star, is an odd resonance of connection to the ancient patterns of the old one's it is heard like a dog whistle and calls one to action of Above, Below, Within. It is a connection to the Golden Pyramid that slips between space and time.

13-Pointed star, is the place we all reach towards into 2012 and beyond. The 13- Pointed Star is peace, and wisdom working. It is a balance of nature, time and space. This is a place where the center of the star emerges into a cosmic consciousness of wholeness for all our relations.

Conscious Choice gives you the right to co-create the future.

THERE IS A STAR THAT IS MY LIGHT

IT TAKES ME THROUGH THE NIGHT

MY GIFT IS NEW SIGHT

MY PATH IS MY JOURNEY AND RIGHT

MY JOURNEY IS MY DESTINY AND LIFTING IN FLIGHT

☪

JOURNEY EIGHT

Wisdom of knowing Self/Celph

IT'S ALL ABOUT SELF AWARENESS, SELF PROMOTION, SELF ACCEPTANCE A SACRED CO-CREATION WITH SELF. NEW WORDS OF WHOLENESS COME.

MEET YOUR WISEST SELF

MEET YOUR MOST LOVING SELF

MEET YOUR GENIUS SELF

MEET YOUR TRANSFORMED SELF

MEET YOUR HIGHER SELF

The next aspects of the journey were presented with a worksheet that I was to make copies of and use as I aligned myself with what each aspect of my own inner dictionary allowed me to know as the truth of my Celph. Celph is the only spirit guide we ever have to rely upon, if we do honor to this inner work. Grandma and Grandpa constantly nagged at me that we all had our ears on crooked and we did not even know our own language.

When it comes to assisting others in transformation one of the most important tools is the ability to know that you are both speaking the same language in some form. You have to have a dictionary of agreement about what a term means and how it is leading aspects of ego, soul and life.

The discovery of Celph had actually happened in my forty-second year, and my Medicine Partner and road warrioress, Lulu and I had a magical trip to Michigan one fall weekend. We were there to offer lodges for the large group of women and do join in council and healing ritual with other well known Elders and a few surprise Grandma's. One Grandma saw our lodge fire from her near by island and rowed over in a canoe and joined us for ritual. It ended up that she was the Medicine Chief's wife and we became loving friends for years to come.

On that weekend, women were asking every Grandmother who they looked to as a Spirit guide or Medicine helper. Lulu and I sat in the lodge for hours looking for our proper answer. Suddenly we came up with CELPH, the one place we always have to look for guidance. By the end of the weekend, we had a stuffed bear named Celph who would guide us on our coming road trips. We laughed a lot with Celph that summer and came up with a small workbook to share with our circles back home.

Now as I was entering my fifty- eighth year (notice, as I write that I am getting older It happens.) , and the journey of working with the Blue Star bundle and initiations had taken over my life and it seemed time to birth CELPH within this workbook. I can look up at a large number of ancient teachers who are above me. I can see the face of Jesus and Buddha, along with Mary and Isis. I can see the keepers of ancient ritual as they have impacted us with the magic of the messages they left behind in Holy script, hieroglyphs, and on the walls of the Temples, and caves of time. I can look to the Elders who actually impacted my life with their special one on one teaching, that are now holding sacred ground beneath me. They are the people like Wallace Black Elk, Grandma Grace, and Twyla. They are the Elders who welcomed us into their circles like Pir Viliat, and Sun Bear and even Timothy Leary. They are the second grade teacher who taught us to make puppets and fed us when we were hungry. They were the teachers who took us on special field trips and magical journeys as we have danced our way through life on earth

There is this other circle of Elders who have impacted our lives the most. They are the Elders of our Celph clan. We certainly don't give them enough credit and sometimes forget to honor them as a part of the magic that takes us to wholeness. I say Celph, because the word SELF is too limiting. Celph is the nature of our inner spirit. It is the image-nation that rules the roost, so to speak. Celph is the inner elf that allows us to make the choices and own what we own about our own personal transformational process.

HELLO ANOTHER MYSELF....

WHO DO YOU THINK YOU ARE?

WHO DO OTHERS THINK YOU ARE?

WHO DO YOU THINK, "THEY" THINK YOU ARE?

SUGGESTED CELPH EXPLORATION.

The Journey of Celph Acceptance

   A time to see your Celph as worthy to take this transforming journey.

The Journey of Celph Abandonment

   Moving beyond shame. What is your shame to move beyond?

The Journey of Celph Assurance

   Taking the first steps of confidence in the process. What has you tripped up?

The Celph Appointed King/ Queen of the Universe

   Taking the power of responsibility. What would you be in charge of if able?

The Journey of Celph Behavior

   Oh my, this may be modification time. What do you think you need to work on?

Connecting with your Centered Celph

   Accessing the inner confidence to achieve all of your dreams. What dream are you wanting to live?

Communication with your Celph

   Time to transmit the inner truth upon which you wish to act...NOW! What needs your attention the most today?

A Journey into Celph Consciousness

   Becoming truly aware of your Celph. Look at you through other people's eyes.

The Journey of Celph Confidence

   Finding' the faith. What do you believe in?

Controlling your Celph

   Finding what needs regulating without confining. What is out of control in your life?

Channeling your Celph

   Who is that brilliant Spirit Guide inside?

The Journey of Celph Betrayal & Deception

   It's a false path of buggers, and they are all of your creation! Make a list of betrayals? How are you going to overcome them?

Celebrating your Celph

Make your good deeds known. Write your own Press Release about your best efforts. What would you say about yourself if wanting the world to see your value?

Discovering your deepest Celph

Somewhere in uncharted waters lives your true soul. What would be the ultimate compliment of your personality?

Celph Assumed challenges

This is for those jump right in there and rescue more than required. What are you busy rescuing this week? Who created the situation?

Honoring Celph Development

Check in on the progress of the original intent. What is your higher goal?
How will you get there in this lifetime?

Time to become Celph Dependent

There's only one person to rely on to bring your vision to life. What do you need to do to take the next best step towards living your vision?

The Journey of Celph Dedication

Honoring your dreams with ritual. Don't quit now, do a word a week, or a word a day. Keep moving, you'll see where we are going.

Exposing your Celph

Time to show your "real" stuff. What would you like to rpresent to the world and what does that look like if you are on the news live tonight doing it?

Exciting your Celph

Now what really floats you boat? What is the most exciting thing you have done? What is the most exciting thing you still wish to do?

Honoring Celph Esteem

Where's the respect? Who do you respect? Who respects you?

Forgiving your Celph

……and all of those who have violated you in a memorable manner. Make a list, and work it. Who did you violate?

A Journey into Celph Indulgence

    What feeds your inner gluten?

Healing your Celph

    Connecting with the source of your dis-ease. Write your story and find your triggers. Be honest. You can burn it when you are done.

Journey of Celph Compassion

    Honoring your needs with grace and dignity. What needs compassion in your world, today?

Loving & pleasing your Celph

    In a manner that no one else can., what would delight you and allow you to know bliss?

Dancing with your Celph

    Live to dance and dance to live. When is the last time you danced? Where can you go to dance in this cycle of the moon?

Fearing your Celph

    That old black magic has you in a spin. What is your greatest fear?

Celph Preservation

    Time to return to your natural state. What is your most natural safe place?

A Journey into the Celph Righteousness

    The boundaries of what is and isn't proper. What upsets you the most and makes you want to slap someone silly?

Uncovering your Celph Image

    Nobody's looking' but you! What would you like to see in the mirror today?

Taking Responsibility for your Celph

    Someone has tooooooo! What needs more responsibility today? What do you wish someone else could fix for you?

A Journey into Celph Revelations

    Life is just filled with bug epiphany moments. What is the most revealing thing you have discovered this year?

A Journey into Celph Sacrifice

This is all about letting go to receive. What are you willing to let go of to find your wholeness and live your dream?

Becoming Celph Sufficient

May you know that you have enough, and always will have enough. What do you think is missing to allow you to live this vision?

Trusting your Celph

Wow, who is the US in the center of this Celph? Is there anyone or anything lacking trust today?

A Journey to the Willful Celph

Come on and get spunky. What is the wildest dream you could live today?

Working with your Celph

Harmony is the goal, so what is out of harmony that needs your attention.

Winning with your Celph

You will always come in first place in this competition. What is the first place award that would let you know you are really a winner?

Altaring your Celph

Ancient recipes for transformation; What is the Altar of your knowing?

A Journey of Celph Critique

You know the biggest one, let's write great reviews for this production! What is the biggest critique of your process right now?

Honoring your Wild Celph

Time for soaring' and roaring'...... How far do you want to drive this bus?

A Journey of Celph Achievement

Honoring the integrity of your Sacred Journey. Let's set up an awards ceremony to honor the efforts of your Celph.

Celph Affirming

I know I can, I know I am...I can, I am!

Honoring a new Celph Alliance

You ya gonna call when the going gets tough? Who are the top twelve people you hold in your inner Trust circle?

Celph Initiations

Confirmation of the Worthiest Celph you have ever known. Have you set up a time for a special initiation to share with your circle?

Exploring your Celph

What, new questions will take you to the next realm?

Becoming Celph Bewildered

What astonishments honor the path chosen? Is there anything still bewildering you?

Journey of the Celph Betrothed

I do, and I do, and I do. When will you do a marriage ceremony to yourself?

Conversations with your Celph

As last, someone who understands you! What do you need to hear to assure yourself.

Celebrating your Celph Ascension

When is the party?

Celph Absorption

What has you distracted?

Applying your Celph

What is the coolest job you would apply for?

Commanding your Celph (with Grace & Dignity)

Who is in charge of this vision, anyway?

Celph Discernment

What needs weeded in the garden of your vison?

Escaping your Celph

What is there to escape, and where are we going?

Journey into Celph betterment

What would make your world better? If you could fix one thing for the planet, what would it be?

Beyond Celph Depreciation
　　What do you most appreciate about your Celph?

Forgetting your celph
　　What needs to go into the trash file?

Celph Inflictions
　　What hurts? How often?

Celph Initiation
　　Say Yes, I am alive! Take your Celph someplace special and celebrate YOU!

Celph Kindness
　　What is the kindest thing you can do for your Celph today?

Celph Medicated transformations
　　So…what are you medicating, anyway?

Journey of Celph Praise
　　Tell the world how good it feels to be whole!

Honoring your Powerful Celph
　　What lets you know you are in your power? Who do you see as the most powerful people who effect your life?

Regulating your Celph
　　What needs regulated? Is it your budget or your time?

Celph Planted gardens of Hope
　　What is in your garden of hope?

Time for Celph Reflections
　　What do you see when you gaze into the looking glass? Look hard and look long? Who annoys you the most? What about them is an annoying aspect of YOU?

Celph Security & Spiritual estate planning
　　Are you prepared for the biggest ceremony of your life/death?

Testing your Celph
　　You passed, give your Celph and A plus!

Your Wild and Wonderful Celph
　　Dance in the streets and celebrate the you that are so wonderful.

Throughout the ages ritual has been the binding force of family and the connection that has created the greater community. Ritual has been created by the masters as a form or coping with the constant challenges and opportunities of spiritual growth. Ritual comes in every form and from every dogma. Ritual is the gateway to the soul as we each reach within ourselves and beyond our selves to connect with something that is called Great Mystery. In many ways, it is the tribute to the multitude of mysteries that keeps us path finding. Yet, all the while there are some mysteries that we just need to leave out there to be tamed by another in another time. The rituals of this workbook have been shared with hundreds in my own workshops and are connected to the rituals of many traditions of healing as they have been passed down through the ages.

It has been my own experience of creating this workbook that each of us seems to do better at the journey when we have some form of road map made available. The rituals in the book are just that, simple, and hopefully clear road maps to a series of questions that would carry us all to inner answers of times through the years, I have found them to provide a different perspective to the challenges at hand, which seem to shift and change as much as I do. Thus, a dozen of you could do these rituals and come up with two- dozen versions of what they mean and how they have impacted your life. They are meant to open up channels of perspective and provide some new ways to look at old challenges and old ways to bring forth a new healing or stronger support system for what is happening in your day-to-day life.

This workbook was designed to assist you in deciding what you believe in and why life works for you on your own terms. There is nothing here to try to get you to change. Change is something you do as a part of conscious evolution, because you have come to know which patterns in your life no longer serve you.

Alrighty then, we are now entering the twilight zone that is filled with as many questions as answers and certainly a million ways to get to a sacred destination. Some Shaman call this work the way of creating a personal Medicine Bundle. Some call it the Quest to come to know your power and the means to tap into your personal wellspring of magical gifts. These gifts consist of tangible items and those that simply live in the ethers. They are called the gifts of knowing. Most of us simply don't know the right questions to ask to get to the right answers. So perhaps this workbook will take you to answers, or at least to questions on a higher level! (come on, you are supposed to laugh now.)

Those gifts happen on the day that you know what you know is really true, and not just for you, but it is a Universal truth and you just GOT IT. The other gifts are symbols that carry the energy of the lesson, or a tribute to the energy of the person who gifted it to you. IE, you have just been gifted with a drum, rattle, special crystal or ceremonial piece carried by another who wishes to pass it on and with it the story, which you will share with others and it will be part of your new be-coming.

So here is the gig; you can go out and buy all kinds of cools stuff at the New Age stores and even in reservation pawnshops. However, it has been my experience, that taking the journey to find, harvest or receive something of a magical nature, makes it all the more magical. The creation of the bundle should be the healing story. The intent of the bundle comes from that which you most desire and are willing to place your passion into the process of a serious creation, thus there is no reason to ever short change the process.

I say this as one who is willing to take wild and wooly trips to far away places to find the perfect tree bark for a healing tea, or a root that will become a new ceremonial tool to share with others. When I am long gone from this earth walk, those tools will still be here, bringing joy and healing to the new recipient. Some how I know that these tools and my own DNA coding within them will supply someone with at least one magical moment that came within receiving the creation of my juice and my own intending. I say intending, as I always want to nurture my intent, and give it love and feed it my best energy in order to see it take life. That is how I have done everything from the creation of the first cable TV network, to the first cellular phone, and I also take this to the oldest form of Shamanic healing, to the rituals of the Rainbow Earth Keepers, which is the lineage of the processes for personal and planetary healing that are offered within these covers.

Each person who works these process will come to the same place, yet certainly will get there from their own experience, needs and desires. Each of these practices is a means to open a gateway to enter a portal of healing. The gateway swings wider for some than others, and the bumps in the road can be real ruts if one is resistant to really doing the work. This workbook has the potential of becoming a very powerful vision quest for you, should you choose. It can also become a bothersome list of things to do, if your heart, mind and Spirit are not in the right place to volunteer to your Celph the desire to grow into your own highest good. To do the real work that takes honesty, heart and real commitment to...yep YOUR CELPH!

Each of us has a day we mark on the calendar as the moment we came to a knowing that we were on a sacred journey. Even though we seemingly arrive on the planet with that knowing; somewhere between birth and adolescence that knowing gets lost if it is not nurtured with a consistent support system. What we then find is an adult circling the choices of possible solutions to a current crisis, which is by nature the precursor to all acts of transformation. The date that is marked on the calendar is actually the day when one wakes up to the knowing that change is the only option. It is a day when one knows they must evolve or die!

[handwritten margin note: carry me to a deeper knowing of my own purpose and unique power available to me]

This workbook is designed to carry you through that transformation with some humor and development of Spiritual practices that carry you to a deeper knowing of your own purpose and unique power available to you. This workbook is designed with rituals to actualize and to fulfill your greatest dreams.

Taking time to work these practices is an act of Celph Healing and one that requires you to give your Celph permission to focus on your purpose and intent at every level. Many of us find the act of caring for others quite simple, however giving that same respect and nurturing to our own physical being seems to take a back seat. In order to know wholeness, one must achieve new levels of Celph healing. In order to share that wholeness, one must be in tune with the inner truth that etches the vessel called Celph. YOU are the catalyst for healing within these practices and YOU are the one who will have to take the journey and be satisfied with the results. You will only get out of it, what you sincerely put into it. You are the only one who knows when this journey has given you the ride into the Celph knowing of the powers of the universe.

This workbook is about moving beyond the comfort zone of suffering and whining our way through the process. This is a guide book of rituals designed to clean up, clear out and transform the day to day into a creation of wholeness and beauty. That creation is YOU. These practices offer you a process of inner discovery of your Celph. Finding the truth of your own being is at the root of the entire process. Do your Celph a favor and stick with the outline and see what comes of the big picture when you have completed this sacred journey. Listen to your soul's call, read the words you will journal, and discover hidden treasures in your relationships with people, plants, animals and the mystical things of life.

Thank you for taking the time to take care of your Celph. You are the one we have been waiting for, and you are the peace we all wish to feel. Right now, right here...today. Thank you for choosing to be a better human being, Thank you for being and Earth Keeper who wishes to transform the cycles of pain and suffering for the children yet to come.

TIME TO MAKE A COMMITMENT TO YOUR CELPH

The gateway is ready and willing to be opened. How are you doing and are you ready to take a dedicated journey of not only Celph discovery, but desired healing and transformation of identifying your "stuff" and working through it in order to see the world through new eyes and live with new abundance, health, joy and wholeness.

In taking this commitment you are asked to look at every aspect of your lifestyle and belief system. You are asked to clearly come to terms with what is yours and what is not yours to deal with and how to get there will either be a wonderful journey of discovery or ..... well, you have the workbook, so why should there be and/or how about, there just is?

There are more than 52 healing journeys in this book. Originally it consisted of a new journey each cycle of the moon. For some of my students there was the need for more. Thus the creation of a new practice for each week was brought forth. HOWEVER, I personally still find it to be most powerful by doing one practice for a full cycle of the moon; i.e. from the new moon to the full moon, then shift to a new process until we are back to the new moon. You can do these practices in order or in whatever manner they call to you. They are designed to fit your needs as you need them, if you know what I mean. They have come together in a form, yet form follows practice, so get there however you get there. Mainly, once you make the commitment, JUST GET THERE, because you care about you and you CHOOSE to do more for your Celph and all of your relations.

There is no right or wrong way to connect to your Celph, just as long as you connect.

THE JOURNEY OF CELPH ACCEPTANCE

Accept: To receive willingly

Acceptance is an odd relationship that changes throughout life. We all are born into a family that most of us find challenges in mutual acceptance of each other at varying levels throughout our lives. Just when we get to a place when we feel that we have accepted the terms and agreement of the life changing opportunities at hand, it seems that someone changes the rules OR our own needs of acceptance have evolved, devolved or are simply throwing way too much stuff in our faces. There is one level of acceptance that states:

'You are on Earth now, and here are the rules. Accept them or not, this is what it will take to get along....so deal with it.'

For some what they must accept is prim and proper and for others it is poverty and violence. Each of us has a mountain of acceptance that is simply expected of us and to challenge the situation would create more challenges that someone must accept. So in many cases, we go through life simply settling for what is dished out with very little question. Like an answer to the question of ; "why is this always happening to me?" is inappropriate or has a clear and simple answer.

THUS, in my mind the word Accept is one of the first real places we tangle with our wants, needs, desires, and levels of fulfillment. I remember as a child hearing my grandmother say, " It isn't what ya want that makes ya fat, it's what ya get!" So here we are, alive, awake and accepting things as they are, and then spending endless years of our adulthood in therapy from what we accepted. MEANWHILE, there is all of these other goodies waiting for us to accept them willingly. There is all of this positive juice that we miss, because we have become so gun shy about what we have already accepted, that we down play the real treasures and miss many of them in an attempt to accept live JUST THE WAY IT CAME TO US.

Most of us travel through life looking for someone with a magic wand to anoint us worthy of receiving the best gifts that life has to offer. It seems that it is easiest for us to accept the struggles and challenges. They are right there waiting for us to shake hands with each and every day. It seems the easy route to the blessings of abundance and goodness that has always been right there waiting for us is much more illusive. Some how we associate the ability to receive the gift of the compliment or the abundance and support for our visions and dreams as something that we must become super human to be worthy enough to receive. Why is it that we tend to accept the struggle first and the reward as a tribute to the suffering. Wouldn't life be easier if we honored the reward in the first place, and left the struggles alone. Jeez, would that mean less struggle for everyone around us? Now there is a concept! Think of all of the time we could save if we went directly to the juicy stuff and forgot that the other stuff was there to hold us back?

There are times in life that we must step back and take a look at all around us and see what is just not right in our lives. We must look at things we have come to accept that are no longer acceptable. We must face the shadow and determine what no longer works, therefore to accept that person, place or situation is not feeding your soul and keeps you from growing forward to become the dreams and visions that keep your mind smiling and allow you the hope of "one day".

That age-old question of what keeps you from having everything or being whatever you want to be is the first place that each of us looks as we begin to establish and honor the journey of our authentic Celph.

THE JOURNEY OF CELPH ACCEPTANCE

A journal of observations and growth

Date of Journey:_____

The things I most accept about myself are: _____
_____

The things I accept about my family are:_____
_____

The things I accept as my Spiritual truth are:_____
_____

The things I accept as my health are: _____
_____

The things I accept as my dreams and visions are:_____
_____

The things I would like other to accept about me are:_____
_____

Today the greatest gift I accept is:
_____

THE JOURNEY OF CELPH-ISH BEHAVIOR

Behavior...to function, or react in a particular way; personal conduct.

At what point in your life did someone let you know that your behavior was no longer acceptable. Can you remember the circumstances and how it impacted your life? That first memory will be the first program on your fix it disk in your brain and in your heart. The moment when you no longer felt that you were perfect, is the beginning place of all forgiveness work, healing work, and certainly the first place to go for the Spiritual attitude adjustment that will allow you to develop new behavior patterns.

Behavior boils down to the perception of what is good and what is bad. An alcoholic certainly has a different perception of their own behavior as well as all of those around them, based on the levels of intoxication. Most of the time they do not see any of the issues of that disease as BAD. The same might be said of the intoxication of a new relationship, and how we seem to go over board into GOOD behavior when we want to impress someone.   The notions of BAD & GOOD are certainly all set by our parent and teacher standards of childhood. What is good to one is not as good to another. Many have been punished for being BAD students and getting BAD grades, when later it was learned they could have done much better had someone tutored them through some learning challenge. Yet, another might be deemed GOOD because they never broke any rules or made waves. They never questioned authority, and so they did not make other uncomfortable, The whole time they might not have been feeling so good inside, but no one knew that, because they did not want to be Bad......and so it goes. Good days, bad days...just having a day is okay, too.

Our environment plays a huge role in our behavior. The average child that watches TV, listens to the IPOD and uses the computer each day is receiving way more behavioral signals from technology than a parent. They are being fed what they see, feel and experience as a subconscious reality, and they live there over 95% of the time. Thus when one is wanting to adjust behavior, there is a vast variety of old frequencies and programs that must be rewired in order for any major healing to transpire. When we have had less than 5% of our body, mind and Spirit stimulated to accept healing, wholeness, truth and inspiration, how are we to find a real balance with the sorting of non effective energies and those that serve us and nurture us into our best and most functional Celphs!

The constant evaluation of proper behavior (in our self and all of those we are responsible to mentor) is a must. Knowing why we behave in a certain way is always in need of clarity. Is your behavior fear based? Is it based in joy and healing? What is your real motivation to produce positive action? What emotions create your most powerful swings in behavior? What is acceptable conduct to you in others....as well as in your CELPH?

JOURNAL WHAT THIS TRIGGERS FOR YOU:

THE JOURNEY OF CELPH FORGIVENESS

Forgive: To let go, give up resentment, to give pardon

Like many of you, I spent years in Sunday school being told that the greatest powers we had been given from God was the power of love, the power of choice and mainly the power of forgiveness. Certainly I had ample opportunity placed before me to express and desire to receive forgiveness. It seemed, however that words are just words and far too shallow to really do the job of forgiveness. I spent many a hour on bended knee speaking every word I could think to forgive others, yet still felt filled with the pain of the offense, the emptiness of the betrayal and most of all, I could still feel the charge that came up when that persons name or image came into my world.

At a point of huge illness, I was faced with the need to transform many layers of old hurt and betrayal. I called one of my traditional Grandma's who offered me some beautiful advice. She reminded me that forgiving was all about the GIVING part. It is an opportunity for us to give away the story that lives behind the pain and to acknowledge the power of the lesson. It is important that we first give away the concepts of our guilt and shame. As long as we hold on to them, their energy takes up valuable spaces that should be opened to the act of receiving and or accepting a blessing, a knowing. Or a wonderful Gift.

To forgive someone does not mean we have to love him or her for the offense. It simply means that we GIVE AWAY the resentment, anger and hurt that makes us ill. It does not serve the highest purpose of our lives to hang on to the past. We need to move beyond this injury so that we might re-create a new energy of wholeness within our being. Once we have begun to list everything we regret in our lives we find that it could go on for days. Reaching back into the past to drudge up the misery takes up valuable time and would serve us no purpose if we were not going to DO SOMETHING with that experience to transform it into a functional perspective of healing. We all need to use that time to create a vessel that is able to release the toxins of the past in order to generate the new healing juices that will create a more harmonious future.

May we all find stronger ways to accept our humanness and grow with the power of forgiveness.

WHAT DO YOU NEED TO FORGIVE TO BE ABLE TO CLEAR THE WAY TO WHOLENESS?

THE JOURNEY OF CELPH FORGIVENESS

A journal of forgiving perspective

Date of Journey:_____

The people whom I most need to forgive are: _____
_____
_____

The situations I most need to forgive are:_____
_____
_____

My own betrayals I would seek to receive forgiveness for are:_____
_____
_____

As I look to the East, what is it I need to understand about those who hurt me, and those I hurt?
_____
_____

As I look to the South, what must I embrace about my tricksters and how I call them in?
_____
_____

WHAT IS AN ONGOING OFFENSE THAT HAPPENS TO ME FROM MORE THAN ONE PERSON? _____
_____

Is there something that I do over and over that offends others and requires my request for forgiveness, EVEN THOUGH, I do not feel that I offended?_____

_____

_____

THIS IS MY TRICKSTER, WHAT DOES IT LOOK LIKE, FEEL LIKE, AND SMELL LIKE AND HOW DOES MY BODY FEEL WHEN I ACKNOWLEDGE IT AS PART OF ME?

As I look into the West, I acknowledge the places in my body, mind and Spirit that require healing attention, and I give gratitude for the tools offered to deal with the need for that healing to take place._____

_____

_____

As I look into the North, I accept the responsibility to give this suffering away. I will give a gift of food to someone who is hungry for all those who left me feeling empty inside. I will give a gift of warmth to honor all of the places that got left out in the cold. I will offer to the universe my own declaration of responsibility to create a new way of being and giving to the wholeness of my relationship with all of those around me.

I forgive my Celph completely for:_____   _____

_____

I let go of the offenses that have left me filled with pain, guilt,

shame and suffering. Today I stand clear and in honor of the

lessons that have carried me to this new perspective and place of

wholeness._____

Make a journal page for every aspect of Celph and begin to explore what it brings up for you to transform. Perhaps it is how you see your CELPH or it is in what power you have given to other perceptions of your CELPH. You must come to know that CELPH, before you can come to make relationship with others or stand in a place of power of wholeness.

SAMPLE PAGE:

DATE:_____

ASPECT OF JOUNREY:_____

WHAT THIS APSECT OF MY BEING MEANS TO ME:_____

HOW DO I BEHAVE WHEN I AM CELPH_____

HOW DO OTHERS BEHAVE WHEN I AM CELPH_____

WHAT IS A SYMBOL OF THIS BEHAVIOR FOR ME?_____

WHAT ASPECT OF THIS BEHAVIOR OR TRAIT DO I NEED TO ADJUST IN ORDER TO BE MORE BALANCED?_____

HOW DO I SEE THIS TRAIT IN OTHERS:_____

WHAT ASPECT OF MY CELPH DO I NEED TO HONOR TODAY?_____

THIS IS WHERE YOU DO IT FOR YOURSELF, YOU KNOW HOW TO DO THIS. MAKE A PAGE IN YOUR JOURNAL AND WORK IT. HONOR WHAT THAT CELPH MOTIVATED ASPECT HAS CREATED IN YOUR LIFE. GIVE IT A SYMBOL, A SONG, A COLOR. GIVE IT SOME KIND OF ACKNOWLEDGEMENT THAT IT IS PART OF YOU!

JOURNEY NINE

Healing into Wholeness

You know the old adage;

RELIGION WAS CREATED BY PEOPLE TO CONTROL PEOPLE WHO ARE AFRAID OF UPSETTING GOD AND GOING TO HELL…SPIRITUALITY IS CREATED WITHIN SOMEONE'S SOUL, BECAUSE THEY HAVE ALREADY BEEN TO HELL, AND THEY ARE MOVING INTO A UNIVERSAL PLACE OF KNOWING INNER PEACE.

I share from my own experience of one who moved through the hallways of the top corporations and into the deepest ceremonial byways of healing and wholeness. I have stood on the podium receiving major awards for leading women's organizations and corporations to top profits. Yet, I can honestly tell you that THERE IS NO GREATER AWARD THAN THE ONE YOU GIVE YOUR CELPH WHEN YOU COME TO A LOVING PLACE OF WHOLENESS. THIS COMES THROUGH FAITH, FORGIVENESS, AWARENESS, COURAGE AND WALKING IN WISDOM. THIS COMES FROM A PLACE OF TAKING FULL RESPONSIBILITY FOR YOUR CELPH, AND BEING ABLE TO SERVE OTHERS.

In this time of tremendous challenge, there is something special that led you to this workbook. May you take many fine moments of knowing peace and clarity as you take your own sacred journey. May the Elders and healers who passed this on through this sacred vessel feel their breath in your wind and know that they are able to support you from the veils beyond.

There comes a time when each of us must look to ourselves for the deepest truth. We can climb the highest mountains and swim the deepest seas as we chase every great master and oracle. Yet it is within the depths of our own hearts that we find the real answers and the meaning of life. We find our light within the shadows of our own souls. We find the soul-utions are right within each of us, when we become still to listen, to feel and to acknowledge that we are the healers that we are looking for.

May this journey bring you deep and powerful awareness of the healing power of the universe as it has for me and all of my ancestors, and the guides who seem to have taken life within my own cells.

It is important to remember that the power that made the body, is the same power that heals the body. In order to really know wholeness we must look at the seed and source of the disease to find the same seed for the healing.

Relax, Remember, Restore

We reach into the magical bundles to find the wholeness. Even when we know that it is within us, we are seeking keys to unlock the gateways that we have solidly closed in our trauma of experience of the past. We hang on to our trauma, at times, like the monkey with his hand in the cookie jar. We cling to the volume of it and the treasure of something that is ours and ours alone. Yet, we call out to be free of the very thing we cling to.

Thus the next series of questions came to unravel my belief system and to awaken me to new levels of awareness. Trust me, by now I had hoped for more answers and fewer questions, yet I was coming to know that that only way to embrace a teaching was to question it as much as we live it. Thus I began the next series of journals attempting to devise some major new magic that would get us all through this, bibity bobity booooooo.

FIND THE PLANET IN PERIL.

    Which part of your inner planet is in peril? *Nurishment*

DISCOVER THE LEAGUE OF SHADOWS

    Who leads your league? *four*

HOW DOES YOUR ENERGY WORK?

    AND HOW DOES IT WEAVE BETWEEN THE MODALITIES OF HEALING PRACTICE?

HOW DO WE WEAVE THROUGH THE CHAOS?

WHERE IS THE INTERSECTION POINT IN YOUR OWN KNOWING THAT YOU ARE WHOLE ?

WHAT IS CONSCIOUSNESS,

    AND DOES IT DISSOLVE IN DEATH?

* WHAT ARE YOU LEARNING?

* WHAT ARE YOU HONORING?

* WHAT ARE YOU ACCEPTING?

* WHAT ARE YOU SEEING?

* WHAT ARE YOU HEARING?

* WHAT ARE YOU SPEAKING?

* WHAT ARE YOU LOVING?

* WHAT ARE YOU SERVING?

* WHAT ARE YOU LIVING?

* WHAT ARE YOU WORKING?

* WHAT ARE YOU WALKING?

What is wholeness?

* What is Safe?

* What is trust?

* What is the right direction to step forward?

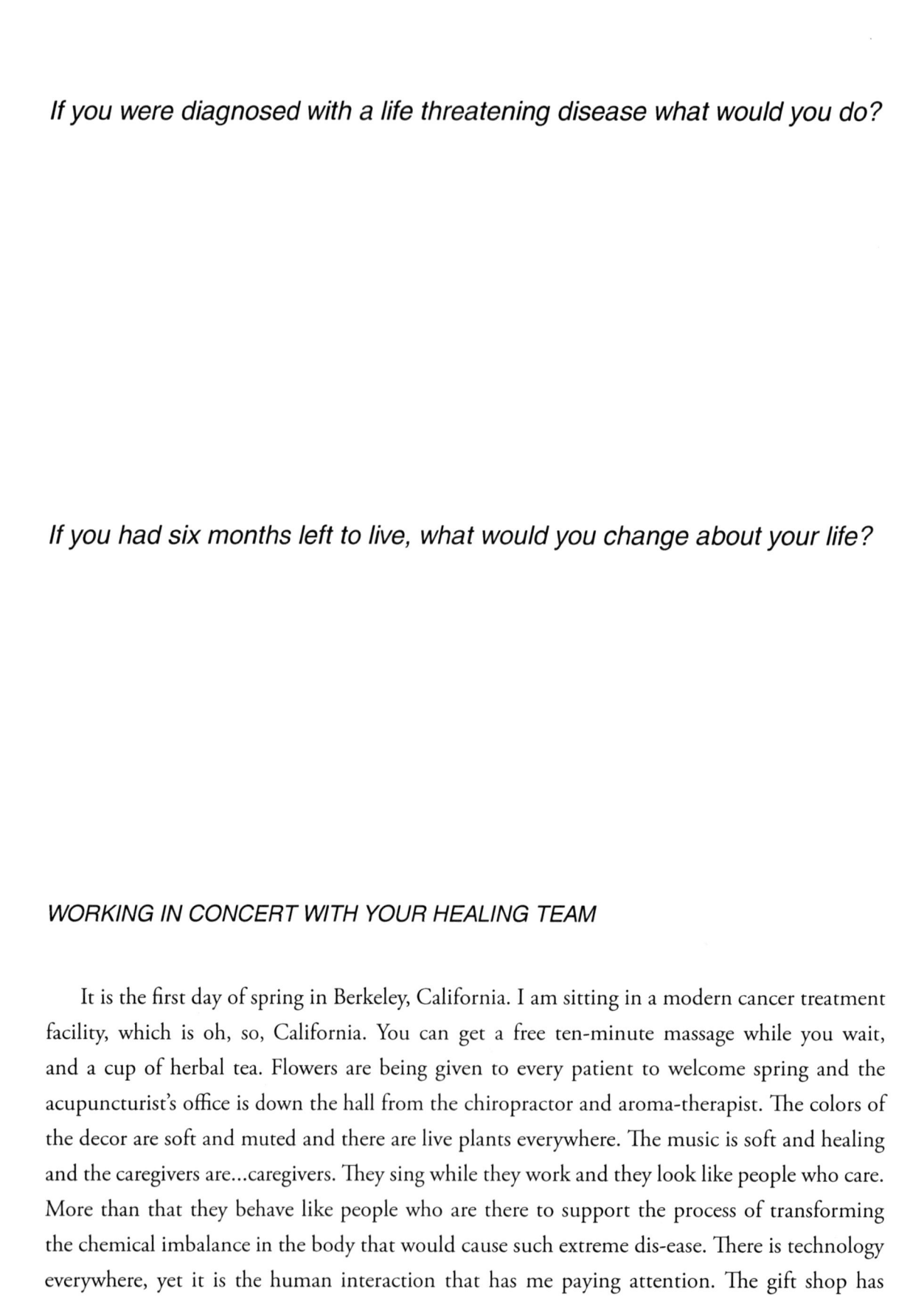

If you were diagnosed with a life threatening disease what would you do?

If you had six months left to live, what would you change about your life?

WORKING IN CONCERT WITH YOUR HEALING TEAM

It is the first day of spring in Berkeley, California. I am sitting in a modern cancer treatment facility, which is oh, so, California. You can get a free ten-minute massage while you wait, and a cup of herbal tea. Flowers are being given to every patient to welcome spring and the acupuncturist's office is down the hall from the chiropractor and aroma-therapist. The colors of the decor are soft and muted and there are live plants everywhere. The music is soft and healing and the caregivers are...caregivers. They sing while they work and they look like people who care. More than that they behave like people who are there to support the process of transforming the chemical imbalance in the body that would cause such extreme dis-ease. There is technology everywhere, yet it is the human interaction that has me paying attention. The gift shop has healing stones, fairies and fun clothing to wear in the hospital. The cafeteria has health food. Even the parking guards have a kind attitude of compassion.

It is like an episode of a TV doctor show. . There are several pregnant nurses. They are planning a baby shower for each other and swapping lists of needs. There are two cranky doctors who are over stressed and throwing out commands that require the ladies to jump through hoops. They smile and skip on to the task they know is the one that will keep the schedule flowing. They wait till they get around the corner to bitch a bit about the doctors clueless demands. There are doctors who are having to deal with the first acknowledgment of having to be the bearer of bad news. There are others who are coming to give a friendly pat of remission and a pass out of this disease, which has been packaged to look better than it feels.

The doctors walk in circles from room to room reviewing charts and asking all of the questions about how everyone should have been managing the protocols. Requesting new tests; many of which resemble some form of ancient torture, others being deemed a simple needle stick and tube involved. Everyone is waiting to hear words like good blood count or T cell numbers. Everyone is waiting to find out when this work of healing will be complete. Some have been at it for so long that every nurse knows the family and patient on a first name basis as well as who is on the soccer team and who is soon to make a career change. Then there are the new folks. You can tell who they are. They came dressed in clothes that were hard to remove and uncomfortable for a day of sitting with tubes in your arm. They came with a concerned son or daughter to help them, or a scared mom and dad. They have a look of terror as they enter this matrix of healing. They have the lists of instructions in hand that are wet from the sweat of fearing the unknown. They actually read all of the papers that are being handed to them to ensure some privacy that will protect the world from knowing that they are sick. As if no one would notice the new turban that covers the patches of hair falling out, or the sallow skin that say chemo is kicking my ass. The new ones make sideways glances at the old ones to see what is being offered as a cure for their pain. Everyone has a story. Some tell it over and over. Others close up in silence and grit their teeth to offer the acknowledgment of this is not how they planned to spend this year. I try to remember to smile at everyone as I pass him or her and offer a silent prayer of compassion. Hoping a moment of my energetic work will make a difference for them, if only for a moment. It is a quiet offering with a gentle knowing in my heart of seeing a face relax for a second or two.

* Dress for the occasion. Wear soft, comfortable clothes in bright colors and engage the healing process.

* Know your medical history, have bottles of all meds with you and know what tests or treatments you are going to participate in, be clear with your allergies and your needs.

* Ask lots of questions and LISTEN to the answers, then, ask more questions.

* Watch what is happening around you. Ask about the equipment being used and how it works and why, if for no other reason than to engage the technician in something that is of their interest and knowing. You will get better attention that way.

* When in pain, indicate it, but don't blame the nurse for the torture of the test. He or She did not invent it, but DO let them know of your own discomfort level, so they can do something to assist.

* When in fear of the tests, the bills, and the results; the long list of things that are filled with fear. Honor that fear, acknowledge it and move through it. Fear cannot be a guide through the healing matrix. Make choices out of solution NOT FEAR BASED RESPONSE. For instance, taking a treatment out of fear of getting a disease is a waste of healing time. Just because your Grandma had it, does not mean you have even lived the same lifestyle. What is does mean is that you need to live a lifestyle that is mindful of the potential that a all substance, anger, shame, guilt, fear and negative charges have an effect on your body as much as Grandmas DNA. Then make educated choices. With the Internet there is information about every disease and potential healing available with an afternoon of research.

STUDIES SHOW THAT A PERSON BECOMES MORE ILL AT THE TIME THEY HAVE CONVINCED THEMSELVES THAT THEY AREA REALLY GOING TO DIE FROM THIS NEWLY NAMED DIS-EASE. The cure to that healing crisis ALWAYS requires for the patient to become an active part of the healing team.

The bottom line is that we as a species have developed more disease than solutions. There are plenty solutions available and many opportunities to honor those solutions as a healing option. Healing requires a team effort, which mean that you are the captain who is deciding who will be on your team and who is playing the same game that you are. You simply cannot win at a game that you do not choose to play and remember YOU CANNOT FIGHT FOR PEACE, so fighting a disease or addressing it as a battle give it a negative charge. For myself I found that embracing aspects of my disease as a part of me was a big help. When I talked to my organs with compassion and not anger and asked it to live with me in harmony was a much better response than going it to kill some part of myself in order to live. The main thing was that I had to make choices and then honor them and become one with the healing solution.

There have been many wonderful rituals of healing shared with me through the years. All of them have involved forgiveness of others and myself and all of them have involved lots of gratitude for the support systems around me. I take a gift to my healing team on a regular basis. It might be something as simple as a jar of jam that I made, but it is always something beyond the money that is required to acknowledge the service given and the healing received. The bottom line, is that we can and should include ritual in our healing. We can and should be mindful of all of the process that is happening in the healing process being offered to us by professionals of all protocol in order to honor that protocol and to enhance it healing journey through our own body, mind and Spirit.

DO NOT BE DELIGHTED BECAUSE OF PRAISE ANY MORE THAN YOU ARE DISTRESSED BECAUSE OF BLAME.

WHAT DOES WHOLENESS LOOK LIKE?

WHAT DOES WHOLENESS TASTE LIKE?

WHAT COLOR IS WHOLENESS?

WHAT DOES WHOLENESS SMELL LIKE?

WHAT DOES WHOLENESS FEEL LIKE?

WHAT DOES WHOLENESS SOUND LIKE?

WHERE DOES WHOLENESS LIVE?

WHAT FEEDS YOUR SYSTEM?

        DISTURBS YOUR SYSTEM?

        OBSERVES YOUR SYSTEM?

        TRANSFORMS YOUR SYSTEM?

    WHAT OF YOUR BELIEF CONTROLS YOUR BIOLOGY?

    HOW DO YOU KNOW WHAT YOU KNOW IS TRUE?

    WHAT ARE YOUR HONESTLY COMMITTED TO?

I personally went through a great deal of nonsense as I answered those questions. Like most, the first series of answers were to impress others with what I was certain I was capable of doing. By nature, I am a big thinker. I feel like I should be able to feed the masses, not just one guest at a time. I am an eldest child and a capable spinner of dreams. Yet, I appear to fail as much and more than I succeed. I cannot turn off the dreaming. It serves no purpose to stop dreaming and creating, as long as it is productive. I suppose the real issue is to decide was is productive and what will satisfy the inner needs that scream for some wild form of attention. In my own case, my mind creates many images I cannot deliver through my hands, alone. I have to add the story or some outside image to help others see what I see inside my own head. When I am doing ceremony or connecting with the ancient sources, it gets pretty busy in there. I find myself having to sort what is practical and what is just pretty or delightful to my soul, but not for functioning among those around me.

Delivery of the message is everything. They taught us that in TV advertising. You get less than 30 seconds to convince someone they need something enough to go into debt to own it. Creating desire through the delivery of images feeds many a business and a soul.

In the Shamanic world, we call to deliver on a different frequency. Wholeness includes the dark night of our shadow visits. It includes the fear and doubt and shame. YET, the goal of the Shamanic process is to transform those old demons into something more functional, more blissful. We must call upon those demons as the tools of our transformation. It is the heat of the fear and the shaking as we remember old pain, and in the pain we are able to recall of the sweetness of the rose. The flower still has a thorn, but we are more focused on the scent of love, than the pain of the thorn that once bit the finger while we attempted to hold on to the moment of the picking. We have transformed a moment of discomfort, by bringing in another series of moments that focus on a color, a smell, and feeling of the soft petals of the rose. All of those moments do not erase the finger pricking moment, but give us more joy so we can hold the rose in a different light. The process of wholeness includes the thorn and the soft petals. It is all part of the beauty of the experience. Now apply that to the trauma in your life, and whap, you have a perfect healing.

Awe, that it could be that simple.

WE REGENERATE FROM THE PROTEIN BASE

Most of our population is suffering from malnutrition. It is the diet and ALL that nurtures us that must be attended to each day.
     …..Bruce Lipton

Most of us are seeking healing answers that are right in our face. We do not need an Oracle to tell us that we eat too much sugar or indulge in addictions that are not healthy. We know it, We either ignore it, struggle with it or find balance with it, after much looking beyond.

For myself, I have always found it easier to swallow my truth if it came with a ritual. I have been addicted to knowing that Grandmothers and wise women all over the world are honoring the same cycles of the moon and seasons. I am never alone when I go into the ethers to seek support for my dreams, because all of the women I most respect are somewhere out there in the ethers conjuring with love and sacred intent. I can feel the threads of my joyful creations take form as I honor all of the other women who are there at the same time. I love knowing that 11:11 means something, and that on 08-08-08 we all did cosmic things together and it formed a message of hope. Those portals of time keep me focused on my own intendings. I have seen this played out as many of us placed our magical intent in portals like the Harmonic Convergence.

My students have come to know that there are certain times of the year, or day or night that I am engaged in a higher purpose to connect with other crazy folks who are engaged with higher purpose. AND, because we all believe we are doing something for a higher purpose, we create it, together. So it works, and that is why I keep doing it. Many is the day that I spend cleaning my home, because it is Solstice and just time to clear the energy. Some folks clean their house because it is dusty, Not me. I clean because of time of the year and the shifting of sacred purpose. I do it because it is time to clear out the things which that no longer work. Which sounds way more cosmic and fun, than the house needs a good cleaning. Period. How boring is that?

So back to Mr. Lipton's statement about that which nurtures us. It is a big part of the magic of transformation. We all put something inside of us that does not nurture. That is part of our nature. AND that very nature is the thing that drives us to look beyond for magical and shamanic rituals and answers to take us back to source of natural being. For most of us it was the sugar filled treats or medications that Mama thought would nurture us that is at the source of many of our medical maladies. That and the many emotional traumas we attach to the treats.

The more ritual I did, the more I realized it was all of the stuff I hung on to that made me miserable and yet, I was the one hanging on. No one else was as much as me. I had not been able to let go of the prizes and trophies that allowed me to validate the journey.

I came to understand that my desire to be a healer meant someone else had to be suffering. AND if I was to believe that we really can transform the planet into wholeness, I needed to work myself out of a job and be okay with that. I needed to stop needing others crisis be my reason for living. I needed to do that just as much as I had to stop hiding things from myself. Oh my, now what nurtures and feeds my soul?

UNIFYING THE MIND REDUCES WANTED ENERGY AND FACILITATES CHANGING THE IMMEDIATE ENVIRONMENT BOTH THROUGH ALTERING ACTIONS AND PERCEPTIONS.

Thus it becomes my job to learn to activate the magical energy to serve a practical purpose. The only thing that seems practical, to me, is the process of nurturing body, mind and spirit in a more equal measure. Thus engaging in magical ritual needs to support the picture of growing corn, feeding your family and supporting your own highest good. To believe that we can have a time of pure perfection in the Golden Age, means that many of us have to be willing to give up trying to fix things all the time.

IF YOU CAN TOUCH YOURSELF, YOU CAN TOUCH THE UNIVERSE. Yep, we are that great.

IF MAN IS ONLY A BODY, THEN HE HAS LOST HIS IDENTITY. So where does all of the other stuff fit in. Where does the cycle of the moon, and the creation of a garden fit into this knowing? Where does the indulgence of the Spirit fit in?

SOMETIMES IT IS ENLIGHTENING TO FEEL THE WORD OF GOD, SOMETIMES IT IS BLINDING. IF YOU MAKE A LIST OF WORDS FOR GOD, YOU HAVE A LIST OF ALL WORDS....and yet we seem to seek something more. We want answers to questions we are not willing to ask. Because all of the answers are as close as looking in the mirror and that is just too easy. We do have a team around us, all the time, and yet we stand in the wallowing of our aloneness and exclude the very essences of energy that got us here. Why do we choose conflict over the ease of just BEING? Why do we look into the tomorrow with some form of fear, when we can just sit in the moment and know peace? Why do we make it so complicated?

ENERGY FLOWS THROUGH ALL THINGS, AND RESISTS ON NONE OF THEM.

Yet we find dis-ease in our bodies because of the times we have created our own resistance! We have fed the pain and the sorrow, more than we have fed the knowing that we have enough and everything is perfect. We have let the desire for more, to become the dis-ease of our time. What will it take for each of us to admit that wholeness just IS!

ABOUT STRESS AND ANXIETY

What is the cry of the human condition that is setting the tone for your reaction?

What makes you move further into the shadows when you feel vulnerable?

What is your loss of breath about?

What is an Altared/altered state for us in this time of our life?

How does the work continue to grow, and what is THE WORK, for you, anyway?

What is the truth of your matter?

What is your PURE POWER and where is it imbalanced inside?

LOOK NOT FROM THE MIND, BUT FROM THE SOUL TO SEEK ALL ANSWERS.

The journey kept making me do the work. I could go to the elements and see how it flowed with water. I could see how things grew with the earth or how they sounded being spoken or sung in the air. I could see if they brought up passion or fear in people. Yet no one could imprint the answer in my cells but me. Others could influence how I imprinted the cells, but ultimately it was my choice as to how I chose to react to information. That would mean to that if I am to transform those cells, I would have to look at the trauma or the challenge from a different perspective. I am the one who knows when I can see the lesson, and not the wound. I am the one who accepts when the cell is feeling better, because I have told it that everything is honestly okay now.

SEE TIME AS 3-D, USE MORE REMOTE VIEWING SKILLS, That was the information given by the old ones as a means to find the Altar that would allow my vision to become reality. That meant to me that I had to look at every situation as if I was looking at a movie about someone else, not me, and then I could decide which parts of that story still belonged in me, and which part no longer served my higher good. Like cleaning my house at solstice. I clean the one I live in and then I clean the one that allows me to live. That is the biggest balancing act of all time is honoring myself as part of the wholeness I want for everyone else on the planet. That means I must live in wholeness and balance. I remember how Sun Bear always signed his books: WALK IN BALANCE. I now knew how hard that was and how special that blessing was that he offered up as a simple way of being.

FIND THE PAIN RECEPTORS IN THE SKIN AND WHAT TRIGGERS EACH SENSE:

WHAT TRIGGERS EACH ELEMENT ? (cold sweats, hot flash?)
WHAT TRIGGERS EACH REACTION?

ASK THE SAME QUESTIONS FOR THE PLANET.

AWARENESS OF THE ENVIRONMENT IS EVERYTHING. Vibration signals create the field for the choices being made of everything. It is all about the frequency that we are able to respond to. Our frequency is altered by certain chemical and states of mind. We must chose which altering is part of our wholeness.

WE ARE A QUANTUM HOLOGRAM PATTERNS OF ENERGY ..... WE CREATE THE MESSAGE INSIDE THE BODY!

The mind is always hopeful, confident, courageous, and determined to stay focused on its purpose. It attracts to itself all of the experience of the elements that will assist in reaching the desired goal. It always looks for a favorable purpose. Do you KNOW when you are thriving? How does it feel and how can you generate life from that essence of THRIVE? You are the only gauge for the brain to give it the command to thrive and to be healthy. Sure a doctor can validate that to s a certain degree, but each of us is the one who carries the command of comfort or wholeness to our brain.

In some third world countries the medical doctor never tells a person they have a terminal disease. The Medical world has found that people live longer, just knowing they have to modify some aspect of their life. As soon as someone tells the mind that it is dying, it amplifies the command and does it faster. From a Shamanic perspective; There is no dying. Yet it is all about the constant little deaths throughout life, until we get to the big transformational death that makes the whole journey such and exquisite ride. We as Shaman should be preparing for the big transition party from the time we recognize that it is all an ongoing death and resurrection show. Our first shamanic death happens when we take our first breath. We continue to grow and shed like a snake all of our earth walk, and probably beyond. So we can ask all the questions we want, but until we live the answers, it is just a series of seminars. We may as well get up and experience the process in every fiber of our being.

WHAT SEEDS OF WISDOM DO YOU SCATTER AS YOU FLY THROUGH LIFE?

Wholeness comes when we: Return the family meal, and read to your children. Tell them the stories of their own lineage.
....Carl Hamerschlag

23 CHROMOSOMES IN DNA

...connect to 23 sacred rituals you have experienced in your life...

1   Birth
2
3
4
5
6
7
8   *Vision Quest I*
9   *Vision Quest II*
10 *Marriage*
11 *birth Karen*
12 *Crone ceremony* — *birth Kristen*
13 *Cancer* — *birth Allison*
14 *Life ceremony* — *Marriage*
15 *Shamanic Death*
16
17
18
19
20
21
22
23 Death

129

What would you change about your life?

What makes you move deep into your shadows when you feel wholeness?

What keeps you from breathing clear?

What alters you to the Altar of healing?

What have you ignored that needs attention?

What is the pain you feed?

What comes from greed?

What comes from ignorance?

What is the dream seed you wish to plant that will grow for generations yet to come?

What is the status of your vision today?

☪

AWAKEN ME
ILLUMINATE ME

    HOW WOULD I SEE MYSELF
        IF I LOOKED THROUGH MY MOTHER'S EYES?

WOULD I SEE THE NIGHTS SHE PRAYED IN FEAR
    AS MY FEVORS ROSE AND MY DEATH RITES PASSED
WOULD I SEE HER DAYS OF PRIDE
AS I DRESSED IN WHITE TO ENTER THE TEMPLE GATES?

WOULD I SEE HER FRUSTRATION OF HOW TO NURTURE
    AND DISCIPLINE ALL AT ONCE?

WOULD I SEE HER RECOIL IN MY CHOICES
    OF MEN AND LIFESTYLE?

WOULD I SEE HER CELEBRATE MY HONORS
    IN THE WOMEN'S MOVEMENT AND MY CAREER?

WOULD I SEE HER CRY WHEN I WALKED IN
    HER SHADOW AND ALLOWED IT TO MERGE WITH MINE?

WOULD I SEE HER RELAX AS I GREW
WOULD I SEE HER NOD WITH RESPECT?

Nicki Scully always reminds us that ATTENTION IS THE HIGHEEST GRATITUDE. IT IS THE COIN OF THE REALMS TO THE HEALING WORK.

Some of us have thought we were paying attention and doing the work way better than everyone else around us. We have thought ourselves rich with sacred purpose, and then allowed ourselves to feel bankrupted by the same standard. The times we have deemed ourselves less than, has not been honoring of the bigger picture. We have not been paying gratitude to the inner guys who drive our own bus as much as those of the guys who seem to be driving the spiritual bus for the masses.

WHAT FORGES THE VEHICLE OF YOUR DREAMS?

What do you need to honor in order to know that the vehicle is heading where you want it to go. Who are you going to trust to drive your vehicle and how fast do you want it to go to get there. Where is there? What does it feel like? What does is smell like? What colors are around you when you get there and what will feed you and nurture you to knowing you have arrived at your own inner bliss?

IF YOU HAD 5 MINUTES TO MAKE A LIFE CHANGING CHOICE, WHAT IS YOUR FIRST TOOL?

WHAT IS YOUR WELL SPRING OF STRENGTH?

WHOM DO YOU HONESTLY TRUST WITH YOUR LIFE?

WHERE AND WHEN DO YOU FEEL SAFE?

The list goes on and one, and it is all part of knowing wholeness. We give so much attention to what we fear, can we give that same amount of attention to knowing that everything is in perfect order. We can manipulate the order through ritual, prayer, altars, and by simply whining so much that we amplify the negative force field enough to demand change. Bottom line, the brain will keep searching until we tell it that everything is in perfect order, as we can perceive it in this moment. It does not have to worry about the order of five years from now, just hold on to this one perfect moment of order and work from there. Wholeness takes action until we come to know it in a peaceful way. On that day wholeness just is. It will always be, because we have come to know it and have made relationship with all that makes us tick and we are feeling the balance of all of the elements within our being. More than that, we are simply happy BEING.

☾★

JOURNAL PAGE:

JOURNEY TEN

Patience creates Big Medicine

WHAT IS A SHAMAN?
HOW DO YOU KNOW WHAT YOU KNOW IS TRUE OF YOUR ROLE AS A SHAMAN?

Now we are reaching into the great abyss when we reach into the Shaman portal. This is such a vast place of controversy and a place where ego and spirit can do a tango for a lifetime. My own have been in this dance for as long as I can remember. Most of us have heard to never call ourselves a Shaman or a Medicine Man or woman. We have been told is someone hands you a business card that says Shaman, then they are not real. So I don't have a business card. The people named me Shaman before the Grams said, hey, own something. You are not Catholic, you are not Mormon, you are you. What is that energy as a gatekeeper and transformer to you? I know that energy to be Shaman. So, I honor the inner Shaman. It is just what it is. And I am it. I am also a mother, a wife, a gardener, a daughter and on and on.

If you are reading this workbook and you are joining the rest of us in the transformation circles; it is a given that you are one of the weird cosmic ones that has lived a lifetime of the Shaman's body of challenge. You have lived in times when you attempted some form of normality and you have always come back to a certain vibration that is your place of comfort. So, I am not going to try to explain to you that I have always been different. I have not. I have always been me. The way of the Shaman came here with me. My mom tells me I was asking to visit the Catholic church to talk to Jesus from my first words. I had never been to a church and she had not discussed Jesus with me. Later, when I was eight I began sleepwalking looking for Isis and the Great Pyramids. I settled for hunting rocks with my Grandfather and the Wyoming Gem and Mineral society until my teen years. My formal apprenticeship into the magical world started for me, as it did for my own children. The Medicine way chose me when I was very young and I hold no regrets. I have served at the sides of many a fine Medicine or Magical master and Priestess. I have been honored to know this as a way of life. I have felt this way and behaved in the manner of the Shaman, my entire life.

For most of you, this writing should only stand as a validation of your own magic and your own journey. That is the purpose. It is the story of many stories as they wove into one. This story manifested when it was time for me, most of us choose to look at our life before we leave this world. This story emerged as I came to know the true essence of myself, by opening a series of old bundles, files and journals that had been held as sacred for women for centuries. I looked at my own life through many eyes, and I had to take a transformation pause to ready myself for the coming Golden Age. I chose to be here now to hold one of the many gateways of transformation. As I prepared for this sacred time I could look through over fifty years of class notes. I could review thousands of rituals offered by the finest Magicians of our time. Yet the one magic I needed to get me through was not theirs, but mine. They left me a road map to return to my source. It was a road map that each of them had to follow at one time or another, because Shamanic death is part of the process. The great act of the Medicine way is timing and synchronicity. We keep moving the energy. We keep calling up the elements and dance and sing and pray, and we keep meeting ourselves in the portals of time. We keep dancing the spiral through space and bump into each other in magical moments of joyful memory. We do this over and over. Yet somehow, we think that it should be human nature to propel the movement with chaos and challenges. In this coming time of a Golden Age that notion is so yesterday and will simply not work any longer.

So what I found out was that I know what I know. I could do the initiations with each cycle of the moon. I could be part of a women's circle that spread all over the planet, and I could be alone in my own process of transformation. When I looked back to see how I answered each question I had to see what effected the answer. I had to look and see if it was the ritual action or the company that was there to mirror for me. The lessons would help me see the real me that had grown up from lifetime to lifetime; all to live this one big moment of being here to be part of a renewal of spirit when the people and the planet were crying out for a much needed change. What tools did I have? What tools do any of us have that will get us through this portal of transformation?

Who will care if our cosmic resume is the coolest on the Shamans block, when it all comes down to feeding the children and growing corn for generations to come? When we all let go of ego and step into that place of knowing, then why do we need to write it all down? At that point do we just BE? And how does THAT work?

And so there you have some of my many quandaries as I began sharing the part about the patience that it took to get to the big Medicine. Many merit badges later, it is all just things and stuff if it does not work to help allow for harmony in your home, in your body and in your workplace. I/we could all climb the highest mountain and do ritual with the Holy Man/woman for a lifetime, and yet it is in doing it for our own family that finally proves our worth.

I wrestled all year with the piece about how to be humble and how to know my own power all at once. I walked the fires, I reviewed centuries of the Grandmother notes and meditated at every power time indicated. I learned songs in many languages and cleared my home on a regular basis. And still, when it came to finding the place of " why do I think that I have anything special to say and does any of this have meaning to the world as we know it…" Oh I could bore you with my mind monkeys for hours. So let's just suffice to say that after doing all of the thirteen rituals to the Shamanic shattering I was pretty shattered. Then thirteen more to a full rebirthing was the only option or die. I know that what I know works for me, and it **might** work for you, but that all involves your level of dedication to the process. Ultimately your determination that it will work for you on some level that allows you to believe in yourself more than you thought you did to begin with. Because, it did not matter who I knew or how many cool places I traveled to seek the information, it was not until I knew that the information was part of me that it mattered, at all!

It was at this time that I began to wonder about every Shaman Elder that I had known and all of the elders that they had known and back into time. Did everyone have times of supreme confidence of knowing this is just who we are and then other times when everything around us is in complete question? I began to look at the years of journals of my grand cosmic adventures and wondered if it was all real, or was I still tripping on that first hit of LSD that I took in 1969? Or maybe I was still in a ceremony in Peru or India. Maybe I was still connecting to a plant ritual of healing that still holds me. Maybe…… It was a pinch myself kind of time. I wanted to validate the years of chasing Medicine dreams and working to support the vision of Elders who espoused to be part of the solutions to the earth changes. I wanted to know that the thousands of lodges, quests, dances and rituals all meant something to the higher purpose of my being. I wanted to know I had not wasted God's time.

Thus I took apart my life, exploring the many aspects of myself. I looked at the questions that the old women had been asking for centuries. Did we all get the same answer? Or is it all just varying aspects of the same reality? How entwined was this event we called life? WHO, WHAT, WHEN, WHERE, HOW AND WHY?

I looked for answers within the questions and I felt what I needed to feel to embrace that as a Shaman I am all of the emotions that are contained within my relationship with the elements and how I express those aspects of myself to others. I can have all of the most magical tools, but if all I do is function in ego, then no one cares and nothing happens. It seems that the real journey is to find the purest essence of your heart to engage the magic of the tools to deliver a less painful process for the next generation that sits at one's side as we grow old.

We teach what we must learn and as I looked at all of the questions and defined what was an acceptable answer, my body got stronger. It had a new knowing in the cells that everything was in perfection. I had experienced moments of being seen and heard as never before. I knew that if I left this planet tomorrow, that I would be okay with whatever memory I had left behind and whatever memories I had cleared to take with me into the next world. I had through all of these rituals sat down with myself and found peace with me. It took over fifty- six years to get the knowing that what I know is enough and that my actions to serve the people include me. It took over fifty six years to understand the real tools of transformation are evolving everyday and have been since that first childhood vision.

The Grandmothers remind us that we live on the thinking layer of the Earth. We share one atmosphere with the Universe! We share that atmosphere with other planets and our aura reaches far beyond the limitations of mother earth.

OUR PROBLEMS CANNOT BE SOLVED BY THE SAME CONSCIOUSNESS THAT CREATED THEM.....Einstein

There is the place of coming to understand that our magic is a constant that spins around us bringing us aspects of the same experience, over and over until we complete with the experience we deem this earth walk. Some of us are working on making sure our cells are stronger in our next birth to where -ever that gets to be. For sure if we are coming back to earth, we have a great deal of work to do to make sure we have an earth that can sustain us, once again. Right now, we need to be as creative as ever in order to sustain in a more balanced manner.

My Sis - Star, Star Wolf, reminds me we can break down or break -through. We are the ones programming the images for our own future. We spend most of our lives recovering from the crisis that we create to perform the task of transformation of lifestyle and situations that we know are not healthy. Most of the time we allow the situation to get so intense that change is the only option, and we spend endless hours in the drama of healing what our instincts told us to avert in the first place. The most damaging choices are the ones we allow ourselves to make out of fear.

THIS PLANET EVOLVES THROUGH THE EYES OF THE VISIONARY. Yet those of us who take pride in holding the vision are the first ones to question its validity. We must believe in our tools and we must believe that we can manifest and co-create everything we need to honor the vision of the Golden Age of Peace. We have all of the tools to know that everyone is fed and healthy. We have all of the tools to know that everyone is a productive part of the community and that together we can thrive. We have all of the tools to work with the plants, animals and balance every aspect of our being into a rational relationship with the whole.

We have the songs, the dances, the rituals that will carry us in full joy for as long as we wish to be here, and beyond. We have enough.

The old ones tell us that radical new powers are actually tapping into powers that existed back in the times of Christ and before. They tell us that these technologies have presented themselves before and it is the most solid practitioners that maintained them and evolved with them through time. There is a blending of science and spirit that allows us to make clear the ability to do the impossible. It has been the means of the visionary since the beginning of time. Life has a math to its wholeness. There is a specific balance that happens when we become the elements and the altar. We become the energy field of regeneration and we can only activate that aspect of ourselves by engaging the heart. We have to care to care enough to become change.

The first seven years of our life we are under the care of others. They are our guideposts and they imprint upon us what they deem important. Yet, each of us seems to hang on to something of our individual nature that becomes the bigger Medicine that we grow into. We dance with each element as it literally co-creates our being with us. Some elements tend to be nurtured more than others, and the places that lack balance begin early in life. Our relationship with the elements may seem fairly basic at that time, yet it is every bit as important as the knowing that we come to in our wisdom years of the importance of making relationship with all our relations. Magic in the first seven years is acceptable imagination.

The second round of seven years takes us to our petulant teen years. By the time we are fourteen, we are transforming our cells and mutating into individuals at warp speed. Our relationship with the elements is heated and responded to with a fury. Our magic has been challenged and we are seeking to find out the meaning of things and figure out a way to control everything around us. Our relationship with the elements and inner spirit amplifies with our accepted and expected growth.

The next phase of the rituals begin to take serious form for us in those years that lead us to twenty- one and adulthood. Our relationship with magic is either turned on or off by then. For the devout, spiritual pilgrim the real journey of the quest is just beginning. This is the time in life that we understand the concept of finding wise elders to train us. For some like myself, those elders have always been there and always willing to share the rituals and creation of the magic. I was lucky.

The years that take us to twenty -eight and our first Saturn return are generally pretty intense. We are busy experiencing everything. We are moving from element to element. We are challenging the magic and chasing dreams, because we are young and we can. Some of us attempt to live the dream and behave within the mundane world all at once. For most of us these are the most stressful years of our life. By the time we complete with this cycle of life, we are ready to look to someone, anyone who might have some wisdom to pass down. We suddenly know that what we think we know is just not enough. By now most of us are working some form of magical dogma. We are into Yoga or meditation. We are into parenting or living dreams. It is hard to know how to get dreams to coexist with the demands of a family. Yet, there is magic happening as we build nests and establish our energy as a valid part of the whole.

For most of us there is a calming and a quickening that comes in this next cycle of seven years. I remember feeling mature and self-assured. I remember knowing that my dreams mattered. I could see a bigger picture that was beyond me and I wanted to be part of it. It was in that period that I joined hundred of wisdom keepers to begin to actually focus the elements and the tools into mindful creations. Anything I had done up to that time had been practice and service to others Only in my thirties did I take on the magical broom of the apprentice and begin to sweep the Temples with some form of self motivation towards becoming a Medicine Woman or wisdom keeper. Only at that time did the concept of living my life in full Shamanhood make any sense to me. Even then, as I left the corporate world, I looked over my shoulder for the next seven years to be sure it was real. In the Shaman's world, WHAT IS REAL?

Only in our thirties do the old ones begin to really share the big stuff. Up to that time, all of the rituals have been preparation. It seems to stay that way all the way through life, thus we must be preparing for an even bigger ritual somewhere into the next world! In my thirties the old ones started to look to me to make choices and to know what they wanted. I had kept a good list of what color of prayer ties each one used for each type of lodge so I would be ready for them when they came to our land. I knew which Spirit foods they prepared and how they liked things facing. Sometimes, I even knew why. I asked a lot of questions and I kept a lot of notes. Soon I had recipes for marriages and funerals. I had five ways to bless a baby or lead a women's ritual. It all took form. Their form as to how they did it and why it worked for them. They learned it from their Grandmother who learned it from her Grandmother and all of the rituals had attempted to remain in some form of original source. Yet each of us put our style into the delivery. It was now someone else's ritual with our style and our intent. Thus it had changed energy in the delivery, but we were merging with the energy of the person who had the original intent.

We became bound by cords of time and those cords became the teachers for a period of time.

The next seven years took us through some rough rides. We knew we knew the work, but the cords kept us committed to someone else's vision. We are still students of the elements, yet taking a stronger role with them. We are beginning to hold the elements with a certain amount of control and we do not always realize that the elements with wrestle with us if we get too cocky. Grandma always reminded me that the minute you begin to believe your own magical smoke, you lose your fire.

This period of time seems to be the big tests of humility and a dance to seek spirit as a bigger form in our lives. This may be as needy a time in our growth as the childhood time. Women are moving into menopause and men are moving into an equally chaotic time of life. The fires burn away illusions and this period of the Medicine journey can be a real button pusher. It is like being too old for dolls and not old enough for boys. We have a bag of tricks developing, yet we are not yet sitting in the place of the wise one, and we are struggling to figure out if we know enough to be wise.

Then we hit that forty- nine to fifty - six period of life. By now we are dancing with each element the seventh time and we are to come to know what it means in our life and how to activate it at will. We are learning to bend time and to manage our aging bodies. We want to do things we could have done in our twenties if we had known how to do them with more grace. We want to dance with the elements and Spirit allies with all we have got, and it seems to be waning. Perhaps it is only taking a rest.

In my own training, I had been given the map of working a new element each year. In the seven cycles of the earth I had come to know myself as a gardener. I had set up recycling systems and learned about toxic waste. I had been a daughter, a wife, a mother and now a grandmother. I had learned to walk slower on the earth and cherish each step. I had learned about the bones, minerals, and stones. I had learned about the Stone People's lodge and the dances of the earth. I have been blessed to be carried by Cannunpa Wakan. I had honored the Earth Altar experience seven times.

Earth who is my mother

Earth of my bones

Earth who carries my footsteps

Earth of my family stones

Earth of the Sweat Lodge

Earth of Cannunpa

Earth of my garden

Earth of my lineage

Earth of Hawkwind

Earth who holds the children

Earth of ancestor's bones

Earth who holds the cycles

Earth made of stones

Earth who generates the healing

Earth of my home

I honor you

As I looked back to define my relationship with air, I had seven cycles of experience. They had ranged form finding my voice as a speaker, singer, and storyteller. I had learned the many aspects of dance and movement. Yet it was the years about lack of breath, or holding breath in fear that had moved me the most. Those were the years that forced me to dance or die. As a Sun Dancer, I have often expressed that I live to dance and dance to live! It was in those cycles that I learned to find power in silence and in walking my talk. (Clearly, I had talked A LOT.)

Every Culture has its sacred voice of calling to the ancient ones. You must come to know the voice of your tool in order to carry its healing message forward. This requires taking time to know your drum, rattle and song. It takes time to practice to know how it will effect the others around you and how you will use it and when is the right time to call it in. It is all about honoring that relationship and surrendering to it over and over. One day it becomes a part of you in all of your essence.

Air of Healing breath and song

Air of voices calling us home

Air of wisdom

Air of light

Air that is gentle and kisses the dreams of the night

Air that is hopeful

Air that carries the prayers

Air that blesses and clears away the fears

Air that is dances both day and night

Air that whips through all that is not right

Air that speaks honor and Air that speaks truth

Air that is compassion that protects the youth

Air that is healing

Air that blows kisses with great delight

Air that gives vision an intended flight

I breathe and I honor you

Fire

Fire was the element that I loved and feared all at once. My seven cycles of fire had been passion filled. I had never done anything half way. I did ritual with a fullness that intimidated others. I took everything seriously. I fanned the fires of transformation with an inner rage that was a demanding task-master. There was never enough in that fire for most of my youthful years. I embraced the fire as a major form of my strength. So much that often I forgot the other elements. I loved being in love with everyone and everything else, but myself. Ultimately none of my Medicine would work if I did not keep that fire of self-love as hot as the rest of the fires I tended. Most who really have known me have come to love and fear the depths of my inner fire. It is a gift that I have had to learn to temper with more gentle flames and a caution when dancing with the winds of change.

Fire of wisdom

Fire of light

Fire of passion that guides the night

Fire of knowing

Fire of delight

Fire of loving and feeling right

Fire of ritual

Fire that transforms

Fire of dancing, questing and flight

Fire of creation and Fire of death

Fire that ends and begins within the same breathe

Fire that haunts me fills my heart with dreams

Fire that heals me and gives my vision stream

Fire that honors with each increasing flame

Fire that twinkles within the candle flame.

I honor the fire that burns inside

    I honor the pathway lit and all who guide.

I shifted and looked at the seven cycles of my own transformation. I had a tear for every drop of rain that had blessed my steps. Water had so much more power than we understand for a very long time. I had watched as the Grandmothers brought someone out of a heart attack with a glass of blessed water. I was certain I would have to use every brain cell every developed to be able to do what they do. I had experienced the waters of birth with my children and the flow of womanhood for forty- two years. I had learned to purify with the waters and to cleanse the soul in ancient ways. Yet the ability to manage each day with perfect flow was just not happening. The tidal waves of energy also seemed to be a constant transformer.

It was not until my fifty-sixth year that I gave back all of the men's Medicine and embraced only that of the Grandmother of my own lineage, did I find my inner Otter ready to be light hearted and play through life. That is what it took for me, and the reasons were prayed over for four years before making the full choice of letting go of what I had deemed my source. I had indeed been on a healing journey on the Titanic. Now I was seeking something a bit quieter like a stream boat ride with a massage therapist and a gentle orchestra to bless my emotions.

Water of my birth
Water of my blood
Water of my baptism
Water of my tears of sorrow and joy
Water of my children
Water of my creations
Water of my cleansing
Water of life, I have known you
Water of the worlds, I honor you

The Metals and Thunders are perhaps the element where the life journey began for me. The old guys used to tell me that Thunder children came every seven years with storms and wars and shifting of time. I came in one of those cycles and certainly had known the power of working the Thunders since childhood. I loved to stand in a lightening storm and call out to the electricity in the air. I got my first shock that knocked me out when I was fourteen. Since that time I have had lightening knock me on my behind a half dozen times. My media work has been a direct connection to the power of the thunder. My stories of how I managed to gather particular stories or be in the right place at the right time, honestly is something that I get from the metal aspect of the elements. I have had mercury poisoning more than once and have found that a mercury retrograde cycle can also knock me on my behind. I have spent much of my Medicine journey learning the alchemy of the metals and the means to conduct energy from field to field. In these earth change days I have been instructed to add several metals to my Altar of intent to merge with the frequency of these times. Those metals are titanium, niobium, copper, gold, and silver.

The Altars of the Stars and Moon have woven within every other altar, but the years that I have focused on them as a source, I have certainly learned some very cosmic things. When I focus on an element, it is the symbols and keepers of that element that sit on my altar all year. It is that element that I allow to guide my Vision quest, my new and full moon rituals and my Altars that I share with others through out a cycle of seasons. At the end of the year, I take time to Quest with that element and honor what I have come to know of it as an ally and how it now works for and with me in my magical tool bag. I never take an element for granted and I am very alert to changes in the elements as in indicator of what is happening on the planet and to the people around me. By revisiting the element every seven years, I gain perspective of the deeper aspects of the element that I did not see the first time around. It makes for a fine study of life.

As for the stars, it was not until after I was in my fifties that our relationship seemed real. I had magical connections in each of my cycles. I had taken those initiations at pyramids in Peru and Egypt. I had made those connections while dancing through the night and around campfires as I sang my way to day- light. Sometime after the age of fifty, the stars seemed closer. When my moon cycle stopped a new channel in my consciousness awakened and I could hear a song of the stars that had never existed in there before. The dreams got more intense and the Altar work seemed clear with intent. I could manifest the shifting much quicker and the pattern of the stars seemed to guide me on a complete new journey. Once the Blue Star Altar was completely activated with thirteen specific rituals, something had taken over my life. Everywhere I looked this work was coming to life. My desk was filled with letters and connections to stories of Elders of every nation around the world. I was not alone in my knowing. I never had been, it just took me this long to catch up with myself!

Great Mystery was the guide to those shifting years. Each time I faced that cycle, I knew it was a year of dealing with my blind spots. It would be a year of thinking I was all grown up and then realizing that I knew nothing at all. I fondly call those years the ones where I was confused on a higher level. In Sacred Geometry the number for ultimate abundance is 28 plus 28. When I finally hit the 56th year, I did feel abundant in wisdom. The need to focus that wisdom towards my sacred intent was the real challenge. Perhaps that is why we call it Great Mystery!

All of this brings me back to another journey with Nicki Scully. Her workshop on becoming the Oracle was quite profound. A group of forty plus women spent quiet weekend sitting in a Georgia field getting ready to meditate. Her set up was two days of preparing a question for the

Oracle that we were willing to go all the way to Dephi to ask. This had left me in a blank space, of :

"WHAT QUESTION WOULD BE IMPORTANT ENOUGH TO CARRY YOU OVER THE RIVER AND THROUGH THE WOODS, AT THE RISK OF LIFE AND LIMB TO SEEK ANOTHER'S WISDOM?"

Knowing of my place as an Elder of her Alchemical Lineage, it was a given that Nicki would call on me to describe what was happening and I was feeling deep embarrassment that I had not even come up with a question. Yet, on the spot, I took the journey. Nicki guided us with her story. As I entered the gardens of Delphi the columns were carved with faces. They were all faces of those that are now on the other side. I walked closer to the room of the Oracle and still had no question. I decided I should present my resume to them and ask them

"WHAT WOULD YOU DO if you had these credentials and had no place to go, but living in Alabama surrounded by the limits of the location and the resources ? "

I remember my subconscious reaching in my bag to gather one of my gifts to present to the Oracle and the Council that surrounded him. As he looked up, it was the face of Donald Trump. I gasped and handed him my resume. He smiled and said,

"Awe, AT LAST MY REPLACEMENT HAS COME!" He then walked off to leave me to meet the others who stood in line awaiting the Sacred answer to their questions.

It is a powerful memory to me. I have spent my life chasing those oracles, when I always knew I had to find the answer inside. I think, perhaps I was seeking a bigger answer and I made it more complicated than it needed to be. Yet, I am grateful for the journey. It has been quite a ride and I look forward to the next chapters it will add to my life.

Great Mystery has been that for me. That energy of creation has been ever present and sometimes just a bit illusive in order to make me raise the bar and reach for a loftier goal. Great Mystery always helps me move beyond myself and allows me to become part of the whole.

On this day of fire I find myself ready to transform my relationships and all that is not working in my family, my community and in my own inner world....I wear the silk robes of change...I am reaching to ANIMISTIC...where everything has a soul....I am standing in Polytheism with the gods and Goddess of all time. I am in the Acadian empire where we will end all witch-hunts.....into MONOTHESISM of the rise of Science. IT IS THE NEW RELIGION OF BEING....

THE GIFT OF THE ELEMENT IS THE RELATIONSHIP THAT YOU DEVELOP TO EMBODY ITS ENERGY AND ARE ABLE TO RE-GIVE TO ALL THOSE AROUND YOU.
 YOU SERVE AS A GATEWAY INTO THAT ELEMENT...

☪

I have surged myself with light and fire

I have filled my soul with Gods desire to love, to teach, to serve
Take me through the night

I feel the dazzling light fill my soul with all that is right open my astral sight sit on my steps and point me in the right direction through my soul, I find new flight.

My love is my light my journey is right take me though the night my gift is my guide my path is my journey my journey is my destiny.....

THE PREDOMENANT MOTIVATION FOR RELIGION IS THE NEED TO MAKE SENSE OUT OF SUFFERING AND DEATH AND TO SHOW US A WAY TO HAPPINESS. THESE BELIEFS ARE MOSTLY CENTERED ON THE NEED FOR A SINGLE INDIVIDUAL TO MAKE SENSE OUT OF HIS/HER IMMEDIATE LIFE AND TO FIND A PURPOSE IN IT. THE FAITHFUL WILL EVENTUALLY KNOW THE TRUTH.

You have a perfect right to be in this universe and to be THIS WAY. It is a basic hospitality of welcoming you to LIFE!

A Reminder from Edwene Gaines

You are the center of the Universe. What you speak, and hear is what is being created in the moment. None of us was clear about that when we were younger and therefore, made some not so great Medicine while we were growing along the way. By the time I had worked through the patterns in my life, I realized that over half of the ceremony I did was to bring some clarity and balance to choices I had made and created with my own energy. I had thumb wrestled with myself through life and needed somehow to figure out how to align myself with a frequency that was more comfortable and applicable to the times. As life would have it, stick around those things happen no matter what you do. It is called right timing. Even though I could look back to see the trail of the Blue Star that lead me here, it was only in this moment that I had a clues as to why it lead me here, in the first place.

This goes around the Medicine Wheel to that patience part. That is the sacred contract that we negotiated when we came in. Some of the old ones told me we could renegotiate, but we can never ignore the sacred intent we put forth the day we chose to make this earth walk. It is within the thousands of co-incidence events that allow us to see that there are not accidents, just lots of breadcrumbs to follow to get us back into the spiral where we last left ourselves!

Oh sure, I could pass one test on how to make a rattle or drum. I could tell you the science and spirit of working with the Stone people's lodge or the traditional tools of my training. Yet the real questions on the test were more like:

Where was I born? Why did I come here? How am I living? Where am I going? How will I get there?

We can make a list of the most powerful teachers in our life. What is the teaching that made them so powerful to us? How is that teaching going to affect our life and those we connect with each day? How are we going to pay that lesson forward?

If we were to make a Spirit box to bury for someone to dig up a few generations from now, what would we put in it? Would we just leave a special stone, or would we write a book about how that stone came to us? Would others care what it meant to us, and the many ways we used it? Each of us has a different way of leaving our story. Each of us has lived it in a different manner. The big journey seems to be about finding the proper menu to feed your soul. In the Shamanic world, you really are what you eat.

In some of the final instructions from the Grandmothers they told me that it was up to me to know how to set up the altar, as I had to feel the energy. They reminded me that the entire journey had been about being alert and paying attention. That I had grown when I had shown strength and courage, That I had only gained wisdom because I was patent enough to reach an age where anything made sense, at all. They told me that the true tests had been about keeping commitments and taking responsibility for my own stuff,

When I looked into my bag if tricks, I had pieces of earth, water, fire, air. I had gathered the metals and the stones and bones of time. It was my experience that bound them together to create new visions. It was my spark of life that triggered the elements to do something beyond creating pain within my being. I had to become internal to enjoy the external.

I sat with the bundles for long hours and remembered some of the hardest lessons. I honored the twenty –eight years of time with the Lakota Elders who carried me through my Sun Dance and Lodge Quests. I thought about how when the old man was dying that I spent everything I had to journey back and forth to care for him. I went for weeks without more than a few hours sleep each night. I served until I bled, yet many was the day that other women called and he told them; " No one is taking care of me. No one cooks for me. No one loves me. No one cleans my house.." I took that very hard, and begged him not to tell people he was not being cared for. It was only in the time of this Blue Star Quest did I understand that in his contrary nature he was telling me that I had to become no one until in my own heart I was someone. It did not matter if others saw me. It mattered that I saw me and honored my own truth.

When I came to know that aspect of myself, I was ready to become SHE WHO KNOWS HERSELF. I was ready to be clear that I had something unique to offer myself and that my journey was not just a series of mishaps, but a well oiled machine that followed the breadcrumbs around and around that sacred hoops until I got back to my own source of wholeness.

Wholeness today meant that as I embrace Earth, I embrace living my vision without fear. That I connect with the waters to bring flow to the work that I see as my truth and my part of the gateway of truth. When I bring in the fire it is to fuel a fire of compassion. I look to the air to allow me to speak with a gentle new voice. I look to the metals to bring my frequency over the wires of the computers. I look to the Stars to guide the dreams and visions to rapid connection to solutions. I look to Great Mystery and I smile, because I know more about less than ever before. And I am at peace with that.

In order to know if the Medicine works for you or with you, it is important to establish whom and what is nurturing to each of us. We need to first establish that we have a valid vision, and then we must put a plan of action behind the vision. Otherwise, it was a good movie we made in our head one day. It had a happy ending and everyone lived happily ever after. Or we did something to work towards the vision.

For instance, one year in a powerful moment, I got word that over thirty thousand young people were displaced in our four state region. Their parents were either in prison (Most of them were in jail on drug charges.) or they were too ill to care for them. The foster homes were full. The orphanages were full and there was talk of placing them in youth detention centers. I began to write letters to everyone I could think of. I began to draw up a plan to build nurturing centers all over the country with a focus on the needs of nurturing the young ones. I wrote up an elaborate business plan that included thousands of volunteers of retired teachers, police, and military. It included Grandparents who needed to be needed, again. It was a brilliant plan. I presented it to organizations all over the country and I wrote about it on my web site. I did some sample programs at Hawkwind and documented the need and what it would take to bring this program to life. I visited crisis areas like New Orleans and I offered support to grass roots organizations all over the place.

This vision was on my altar for four years. During that time I worked each element. I prayed it, I quested with it, and I did every magical incantation I could think of. People every- where applauded the idea and many offered support, once I got it up and running. One new friend even walked it through to the White House for me. I was told that it was a grand idea and would be turned over for Federal Management. The end. No other response was given and nothing more happened. Again, I felt so much passion, I went back to revisit the idea. One day a friend of mine commented on how she was trying to adopt a child and found that the Atlanta court system was so backed up that almost forty thousand potential parents were waiting for a child. That was more homes than displaced children, and even in this moment I had no clue as to how to get the system to be more effective. Meanwhile my research showed that it was impossible to set up a volunteer system without seven kinds of very expensive insurance to protect us from all kinds of sexual misconduct charges. I was told the volunteers could not hug the children and that health codes would have to be met to set up a kitchen to bake them cookies. It went further as I discovered that legal background checks would have to be made to prevent child abusers to join up. The down side of my wonderful vision was mind -boggling.

It was a great vision. I did it a wonderful amount of service. People loved the idea with me. Yet when I hit the wall, it was a wall that I could not navigate alone. When the troubled waters came, I was alone with my vision and lots of folks at the shore hollering "You go Girl." I had to put my time to more productive use. I had to stop saving the children to find a way to feed myself, so I could be there for the children I could mentor, one at a time. I love the few young one's that I mentor these days. It feels more effective than fighting a no win system of road- blocks. I feel more effective and I am taking care of the four that I can mange on my own. That is enough. I am living the vision; My piece of the vision. Now someone else can mentor another young one in their back yard, and sooner or later we will get to all of the many thousands of them that need us. The consciousness of providing that support is my gift to the children.

We each must find a vehicle for our dreams. Living the dreams creates a positive energy that keeps our immune system strong. When we are strong, the entire planet is stronger. You have to live what you believe and you have to believe what you live. You are the only one who can say, YES IT ALL WORKS.

The one thing I got more clear about while doing this project is that as you write it down, and as you journal the experience, you activate the experience in your cells. You take that with you into the next life as a legacy. Perhaps that is why so many of us came here knowing weird stuff and we just got weirder as we got older. YET, the stuff we knew made more sense to everyone around us as we lived it each day much to others amusement.

Grandma Grace used to tell us that all we had to do is "Fake it till we make it!" She was right. When you do things long enough, that is how people see you.

Some ten years after starting the project to nurture young folks, I am no longer spending endless hours writing proposals to agencies. I spend that time with the young folks, one on one. However, I still get calls and letters from many who believe in the idea. I file them away until one day everything shifts and my bigger vision makes more sense. I cannot burn out trying to push the river to make it happen. Yet I know if it is right, one day the Universe will line up all of the right players, and it will just happen. I have done my job. I saw it, I felt it, I expressed it, and I nurtured it. Now I let it grow on it's own. Too many of us give up just before success is within our grasp. We leave the vision for the next guy to discover and state it was their vision first. Think of how many of us wanted to invent wheels on suitcases, before someone actually turned in the patent and made a fortune. It is odd the many reasons none of us filed the patent first. We do that with many of our great discoveries. We see them as more valid when someone cooler than us presents them to the world.

And yet I am reminded by Star Wolf ; "Yesterday's vision, usually becomes tomorrows ego agenda." Knowing that, I still keep having new visions. I dance them to life, and I bury the sad parts of what did not work, over and over again. As I grow to this age and take this journey of Transformation, I have come to know that the greatest tool is my ability to look at the story from many perspectives and grasp the joyful part of what it taught me, and dump the rest in the recycle bin.

As for the patience aspect, on this very day that I write this, I have been at this piece of work for a full year. I had over 200 journals of notes from rituals and life experience to distill into this workbook. Today I saw my doctor who told me that my plan worked. My body is stronger than it has been in the past fifty -seven years. As I move into my fifty eighth year on this earth walk, I know my own truth. I have been seen, heard and loved. I have lived the vision of many, and I am living the vision of my own soul. Right here, right now as I share with you. That is the magic of Medicine and Shamanism. That is the day that it all makes sense. That is the patience each of the old one's finally received of knowing what they know and how it worked in their life. Now I knew what I know to work in my life. *I am keeper of my own vision of me.*

To stir the cauldron of life one must:

Add the ingredients of the soul.

Add wisdom, endurance, and patience

Add honor, strength and courage

Mix with integrity

Transform with the fires of passion

Serve with gratitude

We must change the way we look at things, to look at the things we create.

JOURNAL PAGE:

JOURNEY ELEVEN

Tools of Transformation

The tools of transformation are right in front of us. We have had them all along. It is just that we haven't tapped into them until we really need them. The moment we really need them, we have to take a pause clause in our life contract to find them. In my own journey it had been like that. Perhaps the bigger picture became clear to me, because some old Grandma gave me an instruction to be wise in my fifty sixth year. I wasn't sure I was wise, yet it was clear that I had done my fair share of living and plenty of perspective and experience to share. I followed the instructions.

I stacked up nine containers of years of ceremonial tools collected. These tools of transformation were studied them and I had honored them for several years. I went through the process of questing with them, dancing with them and coming to know them at an intimate level. At the end of the journey and the beginning of the next one was that I had come to know my self as the creator and the created. I had come to know myself as part of the tools.

I went through two full cycles of initiation. I did the thirteen rituals with the intent of disintegrating all in my life that was not authentic and serving my higher good. I offered up everything I had to the process and had found myself coming to the final initiation weak and frightened. I faced every aspect of death and sat at the crossroads of time. I chose to do the next thirteen initiations to restore life, and to connect with my soul's purpose and personal intent. It is hard to say which set of initiations were the hardest and the most magical. I gained deep insights of myself, my fears, shadows and places of light going both directions.

It is today that I sit at the third Solstice since awakening the bundle that I choose to do the thirteen initiations one more time to take me through my fifty eighth year and into my second Saturn return. Oh my, how cosmic is that. It is the journey of centering and reaching out into the world. I would not have known to plan this as a child, yet, it was quite clear today that the act of coming to this place and time in my Medicine was an act that had been set into motion with my first breath on this planet. This third time of working the Blue Star pattern will be the initiations to carry the wholeness of this work forward. This is what the Grams had helped me see about my own journey and how to value what it has taught me. What comes of this next cycle will lead me to the honoring of my original contract that carries me into 2012 and beyond.

They had a sacred intent of finding a way to freedom from a reservation horror of abusive boarding schools, lack of food and abundance of disease and racial imbalance. The men had reached into the warriors bundle and had first fought. Then they danced. Then they learned to count coup and kept the promise to take the blue-eyed children as their own. The Grams, on the other hand went to another place. They vowed to find a way to Washington to change the laws. They vowed to retrieve their own children and bring them back home to the old ways. The had to figure out how to do this while wearing calico dresses, eating government rations, being labeled as "prairie niggers" and treated as ignorant. They had to figure out how to tap into the old ways, and adjust to a society that was not their way. They had to find a new balance. So they looked at what they had in their magical bag of tricks, and it was the ability to dance with all of life with integrity. It was the ability to use the alchemical properties of the elements to shift and transform time, space and disease. The found a way to break through and transform the disadvantages into advantages. They found a way to see the opportunity in chaos and gather their wits to help co-create a new paradigm. We are at that gateway again. These same tools have carried the masters through all of time, and will carry us through the most challenging of portals, if only we pay attention.

FUNCTION EXISTS WITHOUT CONSCIOUSNESS, AND CONSCIOUSNESS EXISTS WITHOUT FUNCTION.

My reality was that I had lived an extra special journey. I had come to know myself as one of the tools of transformation. In this following this process, I came to understand that in my twenty-first year, I had been Grandma Grace's function. I was a tool. She used my television show as a bridge into a world that frightened her. She used my shield to carry the work forward. She never indicated that she even liked me much. She tolerated me, and she taught me way more than I ever knew. I don't ever remember getting a direct compliment from her. I did from her half-side. He allowed me to know many times that he thought me loyal and having passed his wildest expectations. Yet today, as I sit living the same age as those old Grams who allowed me to be their tool, I do not have a younger one to be my bridge. The bridge of these times is happening on the computer. It is happening within the ethers. Therefore, I must become my own tool of transformation and be clear with the fact that as I was born an ether baby, I have certain inner skills to connect to a new frequency. I have come to know that the titanium in my jaw serves a stronger purpose that just allowing me to eat a full meal without pain. I have come to know that the elements play a very strong role as my allies and magical assistants in the process of co-creation of the Golden Age.

It has to make it to a five year plan to be moved into action. Thus WE are the ones that we have been waiting for to write and instigate the plan. We are our own main tool of transformation! It is time now to activate at every level and to allow the magic to happen. We have planted the seeds of change. We have fertilized them with our own shit. We have nurtured them as best we can, and somewhere in the next few years we are heading for a really big harvest. So it is important to weed out that which will no longer feed the soul and nurture the spirit in a positive and loving way. It is important that you respect yourself as that important, and that you humble yourself to knowing…SO WHAT. You just have to be loving and honor this sacred time. You have the knowledge. You have to be still enough to hear it. It is time to break through and live your vision.

Let your life become an expression of your own inner art. Stay focused on the intent and do not get side tracked with others drama. The Universe is offering you a new course of action. Follow it. There is no point in following paths that took you to dead ends in the past, follow a clean new path and see what evolves, trust the magic of the journey.

The Blue Star is a Portal of Wholeness. It is a place of releasing the past. It is a time to clarify your belief and assign the proper attention to your passions. It is a place to rejoice in the motion of your body and the clarity of you mind. Honor the lifetime of synchronicity that got you here, and where it obviously is aimed to take you. After- all, by now you have to have figured out that you are the only one that is going to drive the bus into the next world. Where do you want that bus to take you as you head to the ultimate goal? Where do you want to stop and play, pray and grow along the way? What is the thumbprint you are desiring to leave behind when it is all said and done?

Enhance your life with your actions. Use discernment, maintain integrity and honor the journey. Did Grandma Eve know some thirty-five years before that it would be her Medicine Bundle that would get me to my great Aha? Did Grandma Grace know that I would stick with it and see this vision through when hundreds of others gave up, or found an even better way to see their own vision into life? Did Grandma Agnes know that even though she had no daughters, I would love her in a daughter's way and carry forward her dream of reaching to other women? Did Grandma Coreen know that her Sun Dance would catapult me into building a youth center with one passion and release it with the same passion of knowing of when it was time to let go? Did the long list of women who had touched my life know that they had impressed upon me a serious intent and that they had become my passion along with the children that had been our mutual passion? Did they know? Did we set this up to happen in a council circle many lifetimes ago? Was I doing it all right?

Oh the more I explored the answers, the longer the list of questions became. However, today, this is the third solstice since taking the bundle. I know it to be time to stop exploring the questions and become a working part of the answer. Our society is failing. That is hard, yet, the parts that work, need to be culled out and planted into a new garden. I passed the bundle on to another woman, now in her fifty sixth year. I shared it with all of the instructions and cautions. Meanwhile, I spent the year creating my own Blue Star Bundle. I gathered the materials and made the tools at the same time I became the Altar and the tools. Now I need to know how to allow that Altar to work within the world. I need to put on that calico dress and head out there to become a transformer with a heart. That is bound to be the makings of another series of great stories of transformation.

Yet today, the goal is to share with you the depth of the questions and a road map that you might follow to get to the same crossing point of time. You probably don't think you have enough hours in the day to do this, yet when you sit back you will realize it is doing you, anyway. So you may as well jump in and be an active participant in your own game of transformation. Nothing comes into creation until there is a time of destruction. You have the gift of insight, intuition and a great imagination to help you invent the tomorrows you wish to live. This is a dance that has a new mask, and new regalia. It is a new harmony with the earth and the universe.

Perhaps it is as the young Priestess taught me, change your colors each day. Wear Purple on Sunday, Blue on Monday, Green on Tuesday, gold and Yellows on Wednesday, Enjoy Oranges and Crimson on Thursday, and Reds are for Friday, Browns calm the world down to the earth on Saturday. Something as simple as balancing our colors is a tool of transformation. We enliven in many ways. Another Grandma tells me to put a hematite and a rose quartz in my freezer. Still another tells me to split osha root in my doorways at solstice. It all works. You just have to be open to working with the many options until you find what feels comfortable to you. What worked for me, isn't going to work for everyone. I worked it. I felt like I had no choice. It worked me, so I surrendered to the process, because I had chosen to be a Shaman in every sense of the word.

WE ARE REINVENTING OURSELVES AS A SPECIES TO REGENERATE THE PLANET WITH OUR SOULS.

Grandmothers looked at the tools of the fire, and found it to be a balancing act between their passion and their fear. They had very real reasons to know fear. They had spent a few hundred years being enslaved and tortured. For them to think they had any chance of making change was an act of pure faith. No one believed in them, but them. Yet, they did make change. They wrote grants and used their passion to light new fires of consciousness. They wrote books and continued to light the candles and pray at the Sacred Fire place. They transformed the disadvantage into and advantage. They made lemonade out of their government issued lemons and sold it back to the white man. They used cunning and instincts.

They were also wise enough to use the fire as the power of the cord cutting with stones of obsidian. Back in the day Grandma Grace used to march us out into the woods after a ritual with "outsiders' and we would all clear each other with a small flint blade. Later, the blade and the cord cutting rituals got even bigger. We learned to clear others while cutting at angles and not getting the stuff on us. We learned to smudge it, and cut it with our hands. We learned to move energy quietly in crowded places. In one of my Fire initiations, I entered a large group of people who were running in fear. It was my job to slow them down without saying a thing, but just quietly singing under my breath and moving my hands to slow the energy. I was as stunned as everyone else when the entire group of people started moving slowly behind me, and singing under their breath. Each a different song, but the hum was clear.

The ability to defuse energy is very important to all ritual. The ability to defuse the energy of fear, anger, rage, guilt and shame are life saving events. It doesn't matter how beautiful your drum is, if you can't sing a healing song with it. You can have all the cosmic tools in the world, but if you don't have the good sense to know how and when to use them, they are just trinkets. And still, it is the power of your thoughts, your passion and belief that drives the bus.

The element of air is the one the Grandmothers came to honor above all. It was the power of the spoken and written word. They were able to change the world, by learning a new language and mastering it's power. They then sang more songs, and danced with new insight. They learned to get folks to communicate on the same page. You can't transform a situation that you cannot even communicate. That is also where they found the power of the Thunder. They brought together the passion of male and female, earth and sky and let is blast into new creation. They used their power to inspire others to join in, and they wove webs of connection. They bridged time and space when the only form of communication they had was to reach out and find another friendly hand to connect with and walk forward even stronger. They found a voice that spoke with the eyes and the heart. They found a song that was universal, and they brought light into dark places. Then all of those magical tools did something. And still when they left this world, they took with them, their hearts. They left the same important gift behind, the fruits of their hearts for us to continue to harvest and replant with each new shifting of time. The spirit went with them and it continued to spin in our spiral. They left us with tools, and then they left us with questions. What are you going to transform with those tools? If you only had a short time to live, what would be important to do with them? What will you transform of body, mind and spirit? What relationship or jobs or lifestyle situations do YOU feel you need to change? What are you willing to do to see that transformation to life? When do you know the chaos is complete and the transformation effective?

So the tool of Portal Surfing becomes important in this work. If you are going to do the work, you may as well do it in the cycles and season where it is the most powerful time of the universe. Focus on the seasons, tides, cycles of the moon, and the inner wisdom that calls you.

We have the same power of the universe as God in our individual life. Since we know that God governs the Universe, man will have to govern life. This is always a tough subject; law and life and who is in charge. Mankind as a species is awakening to many new abilities. This is evolution in action. May we all serve to develop the state of separation of mind and emotions and then the blending to find our soul. Then we take that blending and join it with others of like mind and get the work done. This job of welcoming the Golden Age is a WE job. The me, needs to become plural. It is too big for any one person, one religion, one government. It is a one heart, one mind job, and we all need to bring our tools together to build a new paradigm.

All miracles come according to common law, they encompass compassion, understanding and service. We must let go in order to receive, and avoid doubt. AVOID DOUBT and replace it with wishful imagination. That is the beginning of any manifestation. We dream it into being.

MAGIC IS THE SCIENCE AND ART OF CAUSING CHANGE AS AN ACT OF WILL. STRONG WILL IS YOUR UNIVERSAL VOTING POWER.

Evolution brings a responsibility to govern the quality of thoughts that circulate through our minds and to the roots deep in the soul. We are right now setting up things for our next lifetime. Each lifetime we add and delete from some larger contract. I am not sure when the contract is deemed complete. What I do know is that every Grandmother who lived long enough to become a Medicine Altar, had a greater purpose for that Altar. It was something bigger than self, yet knowing that self was big enough to do anything. We have to move beyond ourselves to actually get a clear scan of the situation and the many means we have to apply our transformational skills. We have to look within ourselves to be a certain if we have the skills to meet the task at hand, and if we don't have the skills, we have to once again look beyond ourselves to connect someone else to the vision of our soul. We must move through ego to allow the soul of the project to come to life. Even though the project may have found itself beginning in our own imaginations. Nicki Scully always reminded me that my ability as a Shaman was 25% skill, 25% my relationship with the allies I was calling up, 25% magic and mystery and 25% Gratitude.

I-MAGI-NATION

   I am the magic within

      all transformation begins in the mind

IMAGINATION IS

      THE LIGHTENING ROD OF THE SHAMAN

THE MORE YOU DO,
   THE MORE YOU WANT TO DO
      THE MORE YOU WANT TO DO
         THE MORE YOUR HAVE TO DO
            THE MORE YOU HAVE TO DO

               THE MORE YOU GET TO DO
                 ONE DAY YOU WAKE UP
                     &
                  IT IS DOING YOU!

A TRUE SHAMAN IS ONE WHO HAS EXPANDED CONSCIOUSNESS ENOUGH TO SEE AND EXPERIENCE THE SPIRITS WHO LIVES IN ALTARED REALITY.

SHAMANISM IS AN ACT OF SERVICE TO ALL OUR RELATIONS FOR SEVEN GENERATIONS TO COME...

It is the responsibility of the Elders to seed the next generation. We must move out of the way so that they may live the dream that we planted and nurtured with our visions in action. Find your path, and share your journey.

Spiritual Estate planning

* What are the healing tools of your ceremonial craft?

* Have you written their story and intending, that the etiquette of your personal craft is passed forward intact?

* Do you maintain journals and archives? Who will receive them to carry your story forward?

* Do you have a written copy of your family lineage AND your Spiritual Lineage?

* Whom do you pass your Altars on to in the future generations as someone did for you?

* Have you planned the party of your departing and designed the invitations, and made a Cd of your favorite music and photos to share ?

* What will you wear?

* What foods do you want served?

* Who is on your guest list and have you a gift for each of them?

* Where do you want the celebration held and who will lead your final dance?

* Have you written your Will, Power of Attorney, and your own obituary?

* What is your choice of burial or cremation?

* What is your final Memorial give-away that you will support for the generations yet to come?

* What was so important that it received a lifetime of your attention? How will you play that one forward?

YOU MY CHILD WILL NOT BE TRAPPED OR TAMED.
YOU SHALL BE AN NOT AN ANCHOR OR THE MAST...
YOU SHALL LIVE WITHIN THE WINDS OF TIME.

        Someone important said this. I remembered it.

This all- important tool that was a symbol of your life must have done some amazing things for you and with you. It must have been a tool so powerful that it could grow corn even with no rain. It was so small it fit inside your cells and so large that it sent it's aura all the way into the universe. So here we are. It's the final lap into the gateway of the Golden Age. We are all digging into our magical tool -boxes and pulling out everything we can find.

A great KARMA- NECTOMY, is happening for many. As gatekeeper you can offer them the opportunity to serve the children who need them, not just the corporate dollars You are here to challenge the depression into a transformation beyond medication. You are here to challenge the effectiveness of numbing out a nation, rather than engaging them in solution. Genocide lives within the chemical nature. You are here to bring them back to the earth, which means you have to be here, too. You have to move to a place to connect with heart and soul. You have to join others in the act of moving beyond fear and all of that other limiting stuff.

FOLLOW YOUR BLISS...LOVE WHAT YOU DO AND DO WHAT YOU LOVE...

Prepare for 2012 and beyond. Everyone deserves to Dance into the Golden Age. Prepare for 2013 and beyond. It's a new year that comes with a new cycle of hope, health and knowing.

INHALE THE VISION...EXHALE THE SOLUTIONS...Everyday affirm your knowing of this truth. You are the angel of this message. See yourself in a more angelic manner, and less bitchy manner.

ACTS OF CLARITY CLEAR THE OBSTACLES.

* WHAT PANTHEON SUPPORTS THIS JOURNEY?

* WHO IS YOUR ETHERIC COUNCIL AND WHERE DO THEY COME FROM?

* WHAT ANIMAL ALLIES PROVIDE ACCESS IN THIS PERSONAL HEALING JOURNEY ?

* WHAT PLANT HELPERS PROVIDE YOU WITH ASSISTANCE?

* WHAT MINERAL HELPERS DO YOU HAVE RELATIONSHIP WITH TO USE IN YOUR WORKS?

* HOW DO YOU ACCESS THE TOOLS? Many use altered states of consciousness, which sometimes include pain. Is it Dance, Drum, Lodge, Quest, meditation, breath work, each one of us has a rhythm that will get us there... (even the gases of the dental chair, when journeyed right. I always prepared with lodge, Cannunpa, Smudges and prayer before going in for a treatment. You use what you've got.)

* HOW DO YOU BECOME THE ELEMENT AND THE ALLY ?

* WHO IGNITES THE FIRE OF YOUR SOUL?

* WHO ARE THE TEACHERS AND WISDOM KEEPERS THAT YOU TRUST?

* WHAT SOUNDS, COLORS AND IMAGES WORK TO GET YOU TO PEACEFUL PLACE OF HEALING???

* WHAT IS IN YOUR CEREMONY VESSEL?

* AND WHO HAS ETCHED IT WITH TEACHINGS AND WISDOM

* WHAT ARE YOUR DREAMS AND WHO DREAMS YOU?

* HOW DO YOU FEED THE CIRCLE OF HEALING???

* HOW DO YOU WEAVE YOUR VISION WITH REALITY ?

* WHAT ARE THE SPECIFIC ALTARS YOU CARRY ?

* WHO GUIDES YOUR MEDICINE DIRECTIONS:
    EAST,
    SOUTH,
    WEST,
    NORTH,
    CENTER,
    STARS,

* WHO SUPPORTS YOUR VISION?

HOW DO WE ORGANIZE THE HUMAN CARRIERS OF THE TOOLS TO WORK TOGETHER TO CO-CREATE BROADER SOLUTIONS ?

* WHERE DO YOU HOLD YOUR INTEGRITY ?

* WHAT IS YOUR GRATITUDE A CEREMONY OF EVERY DAY ?

* WHAT IS IN YOUR RHUBARB MOMENTS ?
    Constant Synchronicity ...

* WHERE IS YOUR RELATIONSHIP WITH WATER, FLOW, and EMOTIONS ?

* WHAT IS YOUR PROSPERITY ?

* WHERE IS YOUR HEALING PLACE ?

* Where are the portals of healing

    ....inside self

    ...Altar in home

    ...Altar outside of home

    ...Sacred Sites

    ...access to different channels

* HOW DO YOU ACCESS THE CONSTANT FLOW OF ENERGY AROUND YOU??

* HOW DOES YOUR COSMIC SELF FEEL?

* WHAT TRANSFORMS YOUR FEAR?

* WHAT IS YOUR ULTIMATE HEALING ALTAR... what is in that bundle?

* WHAT IS THE SEED YOU ALREADY PLANTED?

The old one asks:

* What has you confused

* What is your passion

* Where are your pillars of strength

* Where are you feeling present

* What is Honor

* What is wisdom

* Who is Wise

* What gives you any form of enthusiasm
* What is peace
* Where is your gratitude
* What feeds your soul
* What is your plan for manifestation…and what are you manifesting?
* What have you ignored that needs attention?
* What is happening in your parallel Universe

I TAKE DOMINION

I AM WHOLE

I AM FREE

I AM COMPLETE

NOW AND FOREVER MORE

THERE COMES A TIME IN LIFE WHEN WE CHOSE TO DO GOOD RATHER THAN WELL!

☾⋆

Blue Kachina

2012, THE BLUE STAR PORTAL OF TRANSFORMATION

The predictions of the end of the world as we know it; based in the well known completion of the Mayan calendar in 2012 presents a controversy regarding evolution of human kind. Some see it as an apocalyptic time of chaos and destruction . Others see it as an opportunity for a quantum leap in consciousness that will result in a paradigm shift that ushers in the Golden Age. Regardless of which way it goes , 2012 provides a necessary catalyst for complete regeneration and renewal of body, mind and Spirit. A shamanic death is happening for all of us and the renewal of the planet is in our hands. We see a new ray of hope and it comes in a frequency called the Blue Star or the Blue Kachina that has been carried forward by light workers since the beginning of time. As we approach 2012 many of us find a new frequency of energy that is surging through our bodies. We are quaking in the night hearing a call to action, as never before.

Various societies of Elders and other Medicine People, including the Blue Star Council of Grandmothers that I belong to, are receiving many of the same messages in their dreams and rituals. People the world over are being called to wake up and to activate from their hearts this new clear(NU- Clear) energy that is being felt and heard and can no longer be ignored. The Blue Star has its own language of healing and transformation and can be a great resource to align us to the soul-utions that are offered from the deepest source of our souls. The Spiritual call to action is NOW.

Join me as we journey together to activate this new imprint and seek our reason for being. As the Hopis say, we are the ones that we've been waiting for!

A SINGLE THOUGHT CAN CHANGE YOUR LIFE!

SURRENDER & LIVE THE LIFE YOU WANT TO LIVE...NOW!

GET A 100 YEAR CALENDAR...THE ANNIVERSARY OF YOUR DEATH DATE IS ONE THERE SOMEWHERE....

Start your day right
Feed your mind with positive ideas
Use your time effectively
Practice daily visualization fasten your seatbelt everything counts become a living magnet. Action exercises...be prepared to adjust all actions

WAKE UP AND LIVE THE LIFE YOU LOVE...

If you want to change the world...START WITH YOURSELF

CULTIVATE SELF -DIS CIPLINE
DEVELOP SELF CONFIDENCE
HANDLE DISAPPOINTMENT
SHUN OVER CONFIDENCE
ENJOY TEAM SPIRIT
LEARN GOOD SPORTSMANSHIP
CHERISH THE MEMORIES

JOURNAL PAGE:

JOURNEY TWELVE

It's all about FORGIVENESS and GRATITUDE

Okay, so we have heard it over and over. Just forgive others, and forgive yourself and it will al be just fine. You do that. You speak those words, and yet the pain of the trauma is still in the body. You hear those words, yet the pain of the offense can creep up in the night and catch you in an unsuspecting nightmare, just when you thought everything was going just fine. Forgiveness is for most of us a highly overrated word, and sometimes just darn right annoying to hear.

"Just forgive the rape or the guy who beat you…"

We've all been there. Yet, every clinical and lab test shows that when we cling to the trauma is honestly does pad the cells with toxins and can be at the source of most major disease. There are a couple of chronic diseases that they have found that almost every person with it has been sexually violated over and over. Does that mean every person who has been violated has this disease? NO. It does mean that most of us have some form of trauma and life drama that nag us in some lingering manner. Most of us have issues, no matter how brilliant or enlightened we may think ourselves.

In my case when I called the old Medicine Woman and cried about cancer, she said, "Congratulations, you just got that teacher you prayed for. You will certainly know when you pass this class."

She continued to tell me that I had to do several things;

First, she put my organs on notice that they were going to loose their job if they did not get busy. She taught me how to talk to them and she issued them a pink slip and made them work to earn the right to live in my body.

Then she had me take my medications on a journey each day. She had me take them outside with a special cup of water. As I touched my bare feet to the earth I was to face the east and thank the medical world for understanding of my disease and thank the allies for allowing me to understand my body, mind and spirit in a deeper way. I was to make an offering of a bit of the water. I would face the south and thank the tricksters for a compassion filled journey that day.

That, today, all of the medical tests would be clear and prompt and delivered with no p
the tricksters of my own cells would understand that no one wins when I die, so the,
right to choose life and new fire of creation. I would offer some water. Then face the west and make prayers of gratitude for the many healing team players that cared for me. I thanked them for the doctors, nurses, lab techs, and plants, animals and winged. I gave thanks for the healing waters and blessed the thunder that lives in the machines. I gave a water offering and faced the north. Then I would take responsibility for my body, mind and spirit and my commitment to why I should stay here and live. I offered water and thanked earth mother for carrying my steps another day, and sky father for continuing to inspire me. I thanked Great Mystery for miracles and my wholeness. I AM GRATEFUL I AM HEALED, I AM GRATEFUL I AM WHOLE. I did this four times and took my medications with the rest of the blessed water.

The third process was to make a list of every person who ever hurt me that I needed to forgive. It did not matter if they were still alive or even if I knew where to find them. I was to make or secure a gift for each person. This is a process FOR GIVING away the pain of the violation. Each day I took a gift to the same spot on the earth as the medication. I offered it to the east in gratitude that the lesson was clear and complete. I offered it to the south that the tricksters that kept me in anger, hurt, rage, shame, guilt, fear or whatever would now be cleared and we were complete with our dance. I would offer it to the west that the violator received the healing that would allow them to stop violating others. I offered it to the north for the wisdom of taking responsibility for forgiving myself for my part of the drama. I offered it to the earth that I might walk clear of the trauma and to the sky that the toxic memories that clung to my cells would be released. I offered it to Great Spirit with a prayer of gratitude that I have grown further and no longer need this living within me. I give it away with gratitude. THEN, I mailed the gift anonymous to that person if I know where to find them. Or I give it away to someone in need to let go of the ugly part of the memory.

For myself, it was a long year filled with many gifts, and less medications each day. Then one day I woke up and wondered what I needed to do for all of the people that I may have harmed while reacting in anger, fear, guilt and shame. That was another series of connections that needed to be made.

Forgiveness is a life long process. Gratitude should be every minute of every day when you have lived as wonderful a live as I have.

MY ALCHEMCIAL HEALING JOURNEY

Born: **Body part it regulates:**   **Planets of effect:**

AILMENTS THROUGH LIFE:

_____

_____

_____

_____

Need to transform:

What you cannot communicate runs you life.

* What affirmations do you speak to get you through?

* What is stability in your life ?

* What clues have you been overlooking? What is your spiritual bi-pass?

I GIVE MYSELF PERMISSION TO BE STRONG AND FREE.

I LOVE MYSELF ABSOLUTELY.

I RELEASE EGO'S NEED TO LOOK GOOD TO OTHERS.

I begin to take power over my own emotions and find peace within my own body. I begin to take control over my fears and to find a dream to dance with. I make a list of what love would look like at it's finest.

I begin to imagine a person of power that lives inside of me.

I go through the five stages of grief;

SHOCK, GUILT, ANGER, and DEPRESSION, PEACE & ACCEPTANCE..

Make a list of what abundance looks like and feels like in your world.

WHO IS SUPPORT, WHAT IS SUPPORT, HOW DOES IT FEEL? How can you better receive it?

AND OPEN MIND IS A PATH TO AN OPEN HEART. SO WHAT ACTION DO I NEED TO TAKE TO OPEN MY HEART TO HOLD THIS MUCH LOVE AND COMPASSION?

STRENGTH, COURAGE, CREATIVITY. All move beyond OPPRESSION

ACCOUNTABILITY IS MORE IMPORTANT THAN RESPONSIBILITY. Is your Spiritual checkbook out of balance?

Whew, so take a deep breath and sit back. Feel the earth beneath you and join me as we explore the immense opportunity that we are all facing to step up to the plate and emerge into a new time doing the work of each of our personal Spiritual contracts.

I come to join you as a mid-wife to the Golden Age and one who is quite excited about sharing a new frequency and re-birthing process that we can activate as we weave together our SOUL-utions to rewrite the history and her story of this planet.

Eckhart Tolga tells us that we need to be in this moment and everything we need is right here. That is the same thing the Old Medicine Men and Women have been telling us for years.;

Be here now, its not too late.

RESISTANCE IS FUTILE, IF YOU FEEL IT.... IT IS HAPPENING TO YOU. ASSIMILATION IS INEVITABLE, AS IT RESONATES INTO OUR HEARTS AND MINDS. IT IS WAVES OF GIVING AND KNOWING BEYOND ALL OTHER TIMES IN LIFE. THIS WAVE IS INVERTING RESPONSIBILITY INTO ACTION. IT IS A CALL TO INTEGRITY AND WHOLENESS.

We take the ancient knowledge and turn on the high beam of universal love. It is a new economy of Spirit. We must walk forward into a new paradigm without the violence, or the counting coup or the old deep earth frequencies..

We must SHIP SHIFT FROM THE TITANIC TO THE STAR SHIP OF PERSONAL AND PLANETARY HEALING. THERE IS A NEW WHOLENESS IS ON THE HORIZON.

We are now spinning the Alchemy into Spiritual Gold like the women of the Golden Dawn. Each Star connects us to new matter. The Pleiades and the shimmering ones are all around us. Now we are seeing orbs and ectoplasm in our digital camera as spirit energy emerges all around us. The grid works begins to interconnect our lives to our original contract. This process has been happening within other time/space portals like Harmonic Convergence in 1987.

The Seven Sisters who guard the portals Tawamipa oyate are ready and waiting for us to join them in council as we enter 2009 and the time of the nine- pointed star or the Council of all Nations the Eniad.

Even the Dali Llama is connecting in on HYPERLINK http://www.bluestarspeaks.comwww.bluestarspeaks.com a transcendental system of spontaneous healing, by moving energy in the stillness.

It is the call to power from the network of light. THIS IS SIRIUS BUSINESS. The Blue Star Prophecy and the Blue Kachina, the Two Suns are a need seed of light to sprout and burst forward within your spirit. Shedding that which no longer serves makes it so we can get light enough to shimmer through an energetic wormhole. The time for Star walking is now. We look for quantum moments, when everything is spinning so fast, and we stand in stillness. We stand in the eye of the hurricane and know when to grab hold. Some of us feel like we are on a bicycle heading for OZ.

If you are feeling the nervousness in your body, and you want to climb out of your skin, you are here with the cosmic corp. The new junk- science tells us the DNA regeneration is happening all around us and within us. The Old ones tell us we are all working at a cellular level. The black hole in space is within you as well as around you.

SHIFT the song from "oh WOE IS ME, to OH WOW IS ME"....cause everything you ever wanted to do as a spinner of healing and transformation is available for you to tap into RIGHT NOW. Activating a Holy Grail is happening within each of us. As we all come to this frequency old patterns and old tools of our magic no longer work. Our bodies beg to get lighter and react to chemicals and sugars harshly. We are not able to use the same caffeine and stimulants as we used in the past, for fear that we might combust. More than that it is the shaking in the night that makes us feel like we need to do something really important with our lives. We want to feed children, stop wars. Care for old people dying. We want to build nurturing centers and we suddenly want to be nurtured like no time ever before. We want change, we are change, and change is becoming a second by second process for each of us. Holding our mustard so we can do the do is the great challenge. So, according to the masters and first nations Medicine Men and Medicine women, we are not crazy, we are waking up JUST ON TIME. We are all receiving the same visions, emotions and desire to join in service. NOT SERVITUDE, but service to a new system of being.

☪

Put on your favorite journey music and join me.

CLOSE YOUR EYES AND TAKE A DEEP BREATH.....PULL IN THE ESSENCE OF THE EARTH

AND FEEL THE EARTH BENEATH YOU. FEEL THE GRAINS OF HER DIRT BENEATH YOU, FEEL THE ROOTS OF YOUR SPINE LIKE A LONG TENACLE OR ROOT GOING DEEP INTO HER BEING. FEEL THE WARMTH OF THE MOIST EARTH IN THE CENTER OF THE EARTH....

NOW TAKE ANOTHER DEEP BREATH AND FEEL THE MOISTURE OF THE EARTH BEGIN TO ENVELOPE YOU WITH THE FLOW OF THE WATERS OF LIFE. SMELL AND TASTE THE WATERS. FEEL IT FLOWING ALL AROUND YOU AND WITHIN YOU. FEEL IT MOVING THROUGH YOUR BLOOD STREAM. LET IT TOUCH YOUR TONGUE AND MOVE IN DOWN YOUR THROAT ALONG WITH A DEEP BREATHE OF AIR...

FEEL THE AIR ALL AROUND YOU AND CONNECT WITH THE SOUNDS AND THE TONES YOU CAN HEAR IN THE WINDS AND WITHIN THIS SACRED HOOP. FEEL THE AIR AS IT MOVES THROUGH YOUR BODY.

NOW TAKE ANOTHER DEEP BREATH AND CONNECT WITH YOUR INNER FIRE OF TRANSFORMATION. AS THIS HEAT MOVES THROUGH YOUR BEING, FEEL THE EMOTIONS OF YOUR WORLD. FEEL YOUR DREAMS AND VISIONS OF THE WORLD THAT YOU WISH TO LIVE IN MOVING ALL AROUND YOU AND WITHIN YOU......

IN THIS MOMENT LOOK INTO THE DARKNESS AND WITHIN THIS FLAME AND FOLLOW IT AS IT SPIRALS INTO THE UNIVERSE... FOLLOW YOUR LIFE AS IT CIRCLES UPWARD INTO THE SKY....SEE THE BRIGHTNESS OF THE STARS THAT SHINE IN THE NIGHT...SEE THE MULTITUDE OF COLORS SPINNING ALL AROUND YOU. ALLOW YOURSELF TO BECOME ONE OF THOSE STARS AND MERGE INTO THE UNIVERSE.

AS YOU ARRIVE THERE IS AN OLD BLUE WOMAN TO GREET YOU. TAKE HER A GIFT AND HUMBLE YOURSELF TO THE GIVING OF THAT GIFT. YOU ARE OFFERING TO HER, ALL THAT NO LONGER SERVES YOU ON PLANET EARTH.......PAUSE......

SHE IN TURN HAS A GIFT FOR YOU...SHE IS REACHING FORWARD AND TOUCHING THE PALMS OF YOUR HANDS, AND SENDING A CHARGE INTO YOUR BEING......SHE HANDS YOU A COPY OF YOUR ORIGINAL CONTRACT FOR YOUR REVIEW....

IN THIS MOMENT ALLOW ALL ESSENCE OF CREATION...FEEL THIS CREATION MOVE THROUGH YOUR BEING....FEEL YOUR FEET TINGLE AND ALLOW THAT TINGLING TO MOVE UPWARD THROUGH YOUR BEING, FEEL YOU LEGS FILLING WITH ENERGY, NOW YOUR THIGHS, AND INTO YOUR BELLY...FEEL THE STARS SPINNING THROUGH OUT YOUR ESSENCE AND PULLS THOSE STARS THROUGH ALL MAJOR ORGANS IN YOUR BEING. FEEL YOU LUNGS FILL WITH NEW AIR...FEEL YOUR HEART FILLING WITH NEW-CLEAR ENERGY....FEEL YOUR BRAIN ACTIVATE INTO THE SOLUTIONS OF YOUR BEING

TAKE A DEEP BREATH....AND INFUSE THIS GREAT ENERGY OF HEALING OF HOPE WITHIN YOUR BEING:

AS WE MOVE, FEEL THE ACTIVATION OF LOVE.....HOPE.....FEEL THE TINGLING OF KNOWING MOVE THROUGH YOUR SPIRIT...... FEEL JOY AND WHOLENESS.......FEEL YOUR VISION OF THE ONE THING THAT YOU CAN DO TO BECOME PART OF THE SOUL-UTION TO THE CHALLLENGES WE ALL FACE ON PLANET EARTH TODAY.

NOW TAKE A DEEP BREATH AND HOLD THIS ENERGY WITHIN YOUR BEING...AND REACH OUT TO SOMEONE CLOSE TO YOU AND GIVE HIM OR HER A HUG, WELCOME HIM OR HER TO BECOME TOGETHER LETS REACH OUT TO TWINKLE THE WORLD...

I want to thank you for having the courage to find the opportunity in chaos to BECOME part of the great transformation on this planet today. I remind you that the earth mother is going through a Shamanic Death, and we have the opportunity to re-birth with her and to grow new seeds for the Golden age.

I FORGIVE EVERYONE AND EVERYTHING FOR ANYTHING THEY HAVE DONE, PAST, PRESENT, AND FUTURE.... FOR THIS WORLD AND BEYOND INTO ALL DIMENSIONS AND EXTENTIONS OF HARM THAT WILL NOT HAPPEN TO ME IN ANY WAY, PHYSICALLY AND SPIRITUALLY. I ASK THEM TO ALSO FORGIVE ME, AS I FORGIVE MYSELF. I ALLOW TO LET GO TO ATTRACT AND CREATE WHOLENESS AND HEALTH IN MY WORLD AS I WALK IT HERE AND NOW...TODAY.

I GIVE GRATITUDE FOR PEACE, TRANASFORMATION, AND ABUNDANCE THAT IS AVAILABLE THROUGH THE UNLIMITED OMNI UNIVERSE. I PROMISE TO USE IT WISELY TO MAINTIAN THE VISION OF_____ _____
_____

TO CONTINUE TO SUPPORT THE OLD ONES AND TO KEEP THE YOUNG ONES REALLY ALIVE!

WHAT IS THE RELATIONSHIP BETWEEN YOUR PERCEPTIONS... ATTENTION... AND INTENTION??

THE MOST IMPORTANT WORD IN THE DICTIONARY (this week)

ACCOUNTABILITY

Here we are at the end of the year. Many of us have just closed the books on our business so that we may prepare to pay our taxes. The bottom line profits for most is much lower than the year before; at least when it comes to mom and pop business. Yet the bills went up. The cost of living soaked up more than ever, at the same time many a home is trying to decide how to write new budgets and do with less. Hard to do, when ever ounce of stimulus around us measures our worth by the number attached to our credit rating. That's just what we feel when we attempt to place accountability to that which we do for a living, as to how it provides for us, AND what we desire to tithe and invest into our Spiritual and physical future.

Always at Solstice for us magical types, and New Years for the "muggles" is the time of personal accountability. It is when we look at what our goals had been the year before, and sift through the journals, pictures, memories and rituals to see what we did and how we did it. We look to see if we accomplished the desired end result. AND to what end. For some it is a stunning celebration of "Wow, I did it !" We give ourselves an A+ and move on to expand our notions of what we are ready and able to do. We expand our response-ability, because we did so good, certainly we should do more. Isn't that the Great American way? Bigger is better. Debt is Okay, because your credit card company says you can spend more and pay longer; not just physical debt, but Spiritual debt gets accepted too. We tell ourselves that the four major events that we participated in last year were so grand that we should plan for seven this next year. We expand our reach without even seeing if our arms suddenly grew to reach so many new goals. (I have a vision of those multi-armed God's and Goddess as possibly being type A over achieving characters who have been multi tasking through the ages.) We reward our efforts, by overloading ourselves, as if raising the bar is the only way to get to the proper frequency of Spiritual success. That's the years we felt like we got there. Then there are the years we feel we may have failed at reaching our goals. Our measurement for success defined only by the measure of how many flaming hoops we may have jumped through to feed the need to feel worthy of our own dreams. And how do we respond to the moment of failure? Some recoil and hide for a bit. Most jump in there and do just what the successful kids did; they pile on a few more challenges to see if they can do it faster and better than before. The end result in both cases leads back to the center of the Sacred Spiral of ACCOUNTABILITY.

Isn't it interesting that when we overdraw our bank account, someone fines us and reminds us that we are either going to have to work harder, or spend less. Maybe both. There is a serious hand slap and a reminder, that if you do that again, they will charge you even more. Meanwhile, they will offer you a means to go further in debt, as though that is going to come to some form of long -range accountability. It has not worked for our Government. It has not worked in our environment. It has not worked for our educations and medical systems, and it is certainly not working within our internal Spiritual systems. So here we find ourselves, in some level of becoming physically and spiritually bankrupt .

Spiritual Accountability comes as our biggest teacher. We can be too spiritual, and do too much. We can become Spiritual junkies, living from ritual to ritual and forgetting other aspects of life. Folks call us Spiritual snobs. We are. We have loved hanging with the energy spinners of our times. We have loved the Medicine men and woman and the dances of many nations. We have loved the magical journey of sacred portals and healing magic that has been passed on through the generations. We have loved becoming that same magic that we have watched the old ones spin. We have felt blessed when they passed on the songs and the tools of transformation and we have jumped through even more flaming hoops to honor that we were chosen to carry some form of goodness forward. We know that we spent the majority of our budget on the plane tickets, gifts, and magical passports to the great unknown. BECAUSE, that which we have known in our past is simply to funky to want to attach to, and the magical world is one hell of a lot more entertaining. Somewhere between our most dedicated efforts to connect with our soul, spirit and self worth; we seem to look so far beyond the place where it lives. Right where we stand. We look in pyramids and caves. We look to the sky and into the animals and plants around us. We look to gurus and masters and we look and we look. We make grand stories out of the thousands of ways we have made lemon-aid out of lemons.

By the time we have reached 50, we have taken every kind of class from crystals to UFOs. We have been body worked the old way and energized with new technology. We have danced at fires and cried through therapy. (Reasons changing every few yeas as life just keeps right on evolving weather we have or not!) We have been sweat lodged, vision quested, married, divorced, survived parenting that did or did not work. Careers have been changed at least three times. We have dreamed and failed. We have dreamed and achieved. We have been waiting for someone to post the grades to see if we did good and are trying to see how many more things we need to do to get the right ticket to our brighter next life experience. And yet, know matter how cool we got. No matter how many master's classes we passed, we each stuff had to find our own accountability of measuring our self worth.

We have learned that we can be too angry. We can be too drunk. We can be too good. We can be too much of anything, good or bad, if we do not learn to measure balance in some new form of accountability in our lives.

This year I am learning about my behavior as a rescuer, a protector, and enabling Spiritual junkie. I am oldest child who worked in the family business from a very young age. I am a dedicated apprentice of over a dozen healing modalities. I love the rush of creating amazing ritual, even when it is frying my system. I am always sure I can do more. I crave to do something of international reach , otherwise I am sure that I have simply wasted God's time and all of the dandy skills he/she blessed me with to share with others. Shamanic shattering came to teach me better. I find myself having to re-balance my Spiritual check -book and be willing to make more nourishing deposits before I give it all away to others. I am learning what happens when you vision bigger than anyone else could possibly want to live. I am learning, at the cost of my own health. I am now having an opportunity to give myself as much energy as I have been willing to give to others. I am far more boring to work with, for sure. I am working to keep myself emotionally charged about the desire to bring accountability into my body, mind and Spirit at every level.

So as we step into this next great portal of change, may we honor that each of us has much to bring to the party and that no one of us is able or should even want to do it all. We need to have plenty of Spirit to deposit in the accounts of the next generation, and yet hold back enough for our own retirement. We need to pace ourselves and remember that we must be mindful not to take more than our fair share of healing opportunities. There is plenty to go around. Today I pray for wholeness for myself, and my community.

In the end, I returned to the Stone People's Lodge to take my Blue Star Bundle that I had created out of my own journey of Truth and Transformation. I made the proper prayer robes and I cleared the past. I allowed myself to call upon the elements and the allies to infuse the years of the Sacred Shamanic Journey. It no longer needed to make sense. I had long sense stopped asking too many questions and taking a part the 'past live' that had been mine. I had chosen a rebirth year. I had taken my cells on a journey of transformation to find wholeness. The doctors had head shaking moments wondering how I managed to go so low and return so healthy. They reviewed charts to see if it was me, and knew that blood, urine, hair and saliva tests came from the same DNA, yet had completely restructured.

I had taken the Grandmother's instructions and lived them and more. I had embraced the aspects of myself that were Medicine and the parts that just no longer belonged in a Golden

Age. I had played all of the Medicine games and realized that so much of it was just a trick question.

As I completed the lodge and made my final prayer, I heard that old Grandmother ask me one more question.

"Granddaughter, today if you were to climb the highest mountain and swim the deepest sea to find the Medicine Man or Medicine Woman, Oracle or Great Master, what is the one question that you would ask?"

I paused with that as I gathered the pieces of my magical bundle, that I would want to have blessed by the wise one. I sat in the dark for a few more minutes and realized that there is only one question to ask the old one who sits alone waiting to share great wisdom....

"Master, would you care to join me for a cup of tea?"

I would make that cup of tea with all of the heart I could muster, because once it is all said and done; you can have a boatload of Medicine tools, but if you don't activate your heart, you only have a lot of things and stuff to try to drag through a very tiny portal! Get small and give gratitude.

SAHWO NOZ

She who knows the Wisdom of her Celph !!

INITIATIONS OF THE BLUE STAR ALTAR

By now I have an understanding that this Blue Star Medicine has always been in me. The frequency had to change, the poisons in my body must transform into a homoeopathic for healing the greatest bacteria of all, the one bacteria we create on our own is self-doubt!

I did what the old women asked of me;

* *First I made my shawl to acknowledge my own journey as a woman.*

* *Second I made a new fan/fans to carry the energy forward as a dancer of transformation.*

* *Third I made a new rattle to carry a new frequency of Spirit with 32 stones of my own magical journey.*

* *Fourth I added the Blue Star woman to my drum and began to learn the ancient song that had been passed from Grandmother to Granddaughter for seven generations.*

* *Fifth I made seven new pieces of jewelry one for myself gifts for a group of sacred women whom I most honor as my support.*

* *Sixth I made seven new dresses to dress for each altar of my being.*

* *Seventh I made six new essences to anoint those whom I would meet in the coming years til I am seventy seven.*

* *Eighth I connected with the Otter Medicine of my own ancestors.*

* *Ninth I began using a new/old time travel piece with Cannunpa as passed on by Grandma Twyla and received as a birthday gift of my 58th year.*

* *Tenth will be the creation a new Blue Otter Cannunpa.*

* *Eleventh will be the development of a new series of workshops.*

* *Twelve new musical instruments to form a harmony and will be lead by the HANG.*

* *Thirteen is identify Grandmothers will sit in Council as my trust and weaving... <u>I am one of them</u>*

WHO ARE THE OTHER 12????

Upon examining all of the ways I had used my body, mind and Spirit. I was asked to look even deeper into the void. I had to look into the silence and what I had learned by spending endless hours alone in the dark with no one to speak to, nor the ability to speak while my mouth had been healing. I was asked to know my healing team at a deep intimate level. I was asked to look at every aspect of the story and to rewrite it with a happy ending/ beginning of my entire being. I looked to see who, what and where my allies were so that I could actually give birth to a vision that would nurture and sustain into the next seven generations yet to come.

THE WILD IS KEPT BY THE ANIMALS

THE CITIES ARE KEPT BY THE HUMANS

THE SHAMANS KEEP THE WIND!

WHAT RESONANCE DOES YOUR VOICE CARRY INTO THE WIND?

The wind sang a new song today…a song of my heart and children playing in the woods, and a song of sisterhood that carried the four directions, protected the home and blessed the land.

THE BLUE STAR SONG

Wichape Unci, Mitakuye Oyasin

Wichape Unci Pilamaya yelo

Wichape Unci, Wanbli Unci yelo hey

Wichape Unci Pejuta Win yelo

Wichape Unci Okaga Ska yelo Hey

Wichape Unci Pejuta Win yelo

Wichape Unci Wakinyan yelo hey

Wichape Unci Pejuta Win yelo

Wichape Unci Mato Ska ka yelo hey

Wichape Unci Pejuta Win yelo

Wichape Unci Wazi yelo hey

Wichape Unci Pejuta Win Yelo.

Wichape Unci Wakan Tanka yelo Hey

Wichape Unci Pilamaya-ai yelo-ai, Pilamaya yelo Hey

THE BEGINNING

☪

Please join us on line to connect with teachers, retreats, ceremonial supplies, transforming services and support seminars. blueStartimes@me.com

http://web.me.com/BlueStartimes

Rev. Charla J. Hermann

Hawkwind Earth Renewal Cooperative

P.O. Box 11

Valley Head, Al. 35989

http://web.me.com/bluestartimes

Email us: bluestartimes@me.com

WHOLENESS IS AN ACTION WORD!

ABOUT THE AUTHOR

Presentation of Qualifications

Communications Consultant
Holistic Healing Practitioner * Writer * Lecturer
Philanthropist
http://web.me.com/bluestartimes

BIO SKETCH / BUSINESS BRIEF

From a small town family business to a full blown media career, Charla traveled from Chief Washakie Television in Wyoming to the major boardrooms of radio, network and cable television in Sacramento, San Francisco and CNN Atlanta. This distinguished businesswoman has been sought by illustrious American firms since 1972 that have ranged from High Tech to Philanthropy.

In a radical change of personal focus in 1987, Charla moved to the mountains of Northern Alabama, and blended her talents as a writer and producer to follow her dream of creating a documentary series of the ancient practices of Indigenous People of the world. Projects have ranged from the Cousteu Amazon series to practices of the Native Americans and even the

Spiritual and ecological effects of war as was recorded during Dessert Storm. Charla has co-authored dozens of books and films, and her work of promoting Holistic Healing events has gained her international recognition. Her articles have been acknowledged world-wide and a new series of her own books will soon be released in print and video form.

From the time her father turned her loose at a trade show and told her to "sell". Charla has earned the respect and admiration of the business and healing communities. Awards have ranged from Business Woman of the Year, to humanitarian and community recognition. Acknowledged by Who's Who, The Palm Beach Round Table and citizens committees in a dozen States. , Charla aspires to be part of the solution in all of her energetic efforts.

Founder and Director of Hawkwind Earth Renewal Cooperative and Above & Beyond Sanctuary of Hope, Charla can be found working with young families in crisis from the prison outreach programs to all age schools, Universities and churches throughout the nation. Her focus on the needs of the THROW AWAY CHILDREN is the driving force that keeps her raising funds and awareness to support the personal and planetary healing of body, mind and spirit.

PROJECTSACTIVITIESCOMPANIES

TelevisionDeveloped adverting and program concepts, materials and marketing campaigns Radiofeatured in Time, Newsweek, Variety and over 200 radio and television stations Filmsas well as inter-net broadcast on a national and international basis. Charla was a pioneer of CNN, CNN Headline News, and Turner Program Services, as well as President of Four Directions Production Company and Pathfinder Communications.

Her Trade Shows designed, developed and created exhibitions and displays that for Turner Broadcasting, ABC, CBS, Body Mind, & Spirit, Bear Tribe Earth Gatherings, ExhibitionsRadio and televison conventions as well as personal healing retreats provided for Healing Retreats thousands nationwide.

CommercialsComplete script to screen for radio, television and print for clients that have Marketing Support ranged from 'mom & pop" business to the fortune 500 Award winning Cellular series with Charleton Heston and Hank Aaron.

Special PromotionsDeveloped multi-media press kits for all forms of product release, from services to retail and artistic creations of films, books, and video production. Charla has a unique grasp of the entertainment and healing industries.

Public Speaking

Writer/ Producer

Holistic Healing Practicioner

Eagle Altar pg 21